Lost Trails and Forgotten People

Jones Mountain and the adjacent ridges and valleys are rich in history, part of the great drama that has molded the American continent. Here, the story of human events spans more than 250 years of recorded time, from the first settlements of the 1720s to a trail-building era of the 1970s. Before the arrival of the Europeans, Indians occupied the Blue Ridge for 12,000 years.

Most of Jones Mountain is today in Shenandoah National Park. In its remote valleys and wild back country are some forty old trails and traces. There are two sites of prehistoric Indian camps, more than twenty former homesites, old cemeteries, several distillery works, two old mill sites, four abandoned narrow-gauge railroad lines, old logging roads, former pasturelands and cultivated fields now grown over, and the site of a military encampment. This book is the story of the mountain and the people who lived there, left their mark, and died there.

Lost Trails
and
Forgotten People

The Story of Jones Mountain

by Tom Floyd

The Potomac Appalachian Trail Club
118 Park Street, S.E.
Vienna, VA 22180
www.patc.net

ISBN 0-915746-21-2
Library of Congress Catalogue Card Number: 81-81883

2nd edition, revised. 1985

The poems ''The Last Tuesday of Winter'' and ''The Quiet Land'' © 1981
by V.E. Townsend. Used by permission.
The poem ''And by God's Grace'' by Edward A. Bacon. Used by permission of
Dolly Hawkins Seekford.

Cover Photo by V.E. Townsend.

Acknowledgments

I express grateful appreciation to the following people who assisted during the preparation of this book: Jeannie Light, who arranged and recorded several of the interviews; Dolly Seekford, who permitted the use of a recording of conversations between her father, Buck Hawkins, and Edward A. Bacon in 1961 and 1962; Jack Kiernan, who copied and developed many of the old photographs which appear in the book; Robert Schenk, who reviewed the manuscript and offered suggestions; and the many people whose names are listed at the end of the book, who provided information and recollections used as source material.

I especially appreciate the assistance of Carolyn Reeder, my editor, whose support, patience, and attention to detail have made this book possible.

Tom Floyd

Table of Contents

Part I

Planters and Mountaineers

The mountain is an immense
White crystal of ice and diffused light
Under the cold stare of winter's sun.
In the quiet before the sun
Arches above the distant ridge,
There is this simple truth:
The hills and valleys are forever
And the infinitesimal
Scratches we trace into the earth
And the tears we shed will vanish,
And any memory of us will
Disappear like the last traces
Of snow in spring rain.

"The Last Tuesday of Winter"
by V. E. Townsend

On a clear summer day in the year 1939, a dump truck lumbered up the old county road from Graves Mill at the base of Jones Mountain. Two government men were in the cab of the truck. As they turned up the Staunton River Road, they passed the charred remains of burned-out buildings and sheds, what was once Brown's Camp and the home place of Dave Breeden. A half mile up the road at the edge of a field, they passed the burned ruins of more buildings and sheds, all that remained of the old Lillard place.

The road bent to the north and came eventually to a spur leading to the right, down to a ford across the gravel-bottom Staunton River. The driver gunned the engine, and the truck lunged across the narrow stream and climbed a road to a sloping field across from the high cliffs of Bear Church Rock. They pulled up to a white, two-storied, weather-board house with rock chimneys at each end and a grape arbor out front. A barn, a springhouse, and several sheds were off to the side.

A woman who had been watching the truck approach came out onto the porch, and the driver said, "Mrs. Shifflett, we're going to have to load up your furniture and move you. We want you to leave because we're going to have to burn your house down, and we don't want you to have to see it."

Suzie Shifflett had known for days that the truck was coming, and she was ready. "It's all right with me," she said with resignation. "We're ready to leave."

The government men loaded the household goods and helped Dewey and Suzie Shifflett move to a new home several miles away. Then the men set fire to the house and the outbuildings, and within a few hours all that remained were two naked chimneys standing like skeletons, a pile of ashes where smoke was still rising, and a 1927 Chevrolet automobile that was abandoned in the front yard.

The men had finished their job. They had moved out the last family and burned the last house in this part of the Blue Ridge Mountains. From that day forth, the land would return to the wild, part of the new Shenandoah National Park.

11

The Jones Mountain Story

The story of the people of Jones Mountain began more than 200 years earlier, when the first trailblazers of the American frontier hacked their way through the forest and staked out homesites in the unexplored valleys and hollows of what was known then as the Great Mountains. Their arrival came with the first slow tide of British immigrants from the coastal lowlands of Virginia.

This is a history of people with class. For nearly 150 years, the mountain was buffered by big tobacco plantations in the Graves Mill Valley. The influence of the plantations and their owners ran deep in the history of Jones Mountain. For some ninety years after the first settlements, most of the mountain was owned by valley planters. Slavery was part of the routine of life. Even some of the settlers on the smaller tracts in the Staunton River Valley owned slaves. Squatters generally stayed out. Anyone who dared to settle in the area ended up in jail for cutting timber that did not belong to him.

The people were, for the most part, good stewards of the land and good farmers. One tract of a thousand acres has remained to this day a primeval wilderness, a place where houses were never built and trees were never cut. That record was corrupted only by the United States government, which pushed a maintenance road through a forest of ancient hemlocks and giant white oaks. Later, the National Park Service did some timbering in the area, which accounts for the still-existing stumps, but the loggers cut only the dead standing chestnuts (killed by a blight) to make lumber for the cabins and the lodge at Big Meadows.

There were abuses by the settlers, of course, including market hunting and the destruction of wildlife species. By the late nineteenth century, most of the wildlife was gone. One man who lived thirty-seven years in the Staunton River Valley in the early 1900s had never seen a deer or a bear. "We didn't have any deer trails in those days," he said.

Hard times came to the area after the Civil War. Former slaves and their descendants gravitated to better jobs in the cities, and by 1900, few blacks remained in the area. Mountain economics depended heavily on chestnuts and apples, which were shipped 18 miles by wagon to a rail line at Somerset. For years, pippin apples from Jones Mountain wound up in warehouses in Liverpool, England. Some of the apples went to bonded distilleries located on both sides of Jones Mountain, where operators wrung profits from apple brandy, which they sold wholesale and shipped in bulk.

Rye, corn, and buckwheat were basic crops needed to sustain life in the era of the mountaineer. Because the new reapers and threshing machines were impractical in the mountains—too expensive to buy and impossible to operate on the steep and bumpy terrain of mountain farms—the farmers harvested and threshed their grain by hand, just as farmers had done in Biblical times.

A lot of rye and some of the apples were taken into the back hollows of Jones Mountain, where a few stills were operated. For years, the best moonshining was in a secluded hollow high on Jones Mountain, at a site known today as the Jones Mountain Cabin. Part of the history that is recounted in this book is the story of the Jones Mountain Cabin and the parcel of land upon which it stands.

In the course of 321 years, the land where this cabin stands has passed through nineteen owners, beginning with King Charles II of England and ending with the United States of America, which holds title for Shenandoah National Park. The first local owner, Zachary Lewis, held the land for about thirty years, selling in 1784. The last and current owner, the United States government, has held title since 1937. Far out in front in length of tenure were four members of the Nichols family, who owned the place just short of ninety years. When it was acquired by the government in the 1930s, the land was still known as the Davey Nichols Place, although Harvey Nichols had lived there for most of seventy years.

To some extent, Harvey Nichols—a rugged individualist, farmer, and moonshiner—reflected the changes that had occurred since the days of elegance 150 years earlier, when Sarah Dulaney Graves, a planter's wife in the valley, was addressed as "My Lady." Yet, in his own way, Harvey Nichols outclassed everyone in the long history of the area, rising from the status of an outcast son to become in his lifetime the most famous—if not the most admired—resident of Graves Mill. In death, he has become a legend.

The Forest Primeval

In the last days of the primeval wilderness, before the first thud of horses' hooves reached the Graves Mill valley, Jones Mountain stood wild and rugged above a pristine valley, a picture book of majestic scenery. Elk and buffalo grazed in burnt clearings. Mountain lions occasionally stalked through the woods. Wolves roamed in packs. Indians hunted the woodlands and may have camped near the streams.

From the base of the foothills, the mountain soared to ragged cliffs, rock ridges, and a ranging tableland mantled with giant chestnut trees,

13

oaks, and mountain laurel. From the tableland, the mountain branched outward in three directions: Bluff Mountain to the south, Bear Church Rock to the north and east, and the western summit at Cat Knob. Promontories and knolls dropped steeply into a complex network of hollows.

The summit, Cat Knob, was itself a modest feature, deep in the highlands of the Blue Ridge Mountains, sometimes lost in a misty haze. More inspiring were the outreaching arms of Bluff Mountain and Bear Church Rock. For scenic ruggedness, there was no match for Bluff Mountain, where high rock walls poked in relief above the valley. The monumental Bear Church Rock loomed above the forested Staunton River Valley. Indians, whose artifacts have been found in the surrounding mountains and valleys, surely stood on the Rock to take in the soul-stirring views that scanned the wilderness valley and an endless range of jagged backbone mountains and peaks. On still days, the silence was broken only by the faint drone of the river on its rocky course more than a thousand feet below.

On the north side of Jones Mountain, all of the hollows and streams dropped into the magnificent Staunton River Valley. The headwaters in the upper valley flowed from a towering forest of ancient hemlocks, where the morning sun filtered through the branches, bringing patches of light to beds of trillium. Along its five-mile course, the Staunton River was transformed from a ripple at the headsprings to a roaring wild cascade, reaching full pitch at waterfalls in the lower hemlocks. A quieter interlude followed as the stream dropped to the middle valley, where brook trout streaked across deep pools and shallow riffles. The river ended its journey with another roar, plunging over rocks and boulders in the lower valley before flowing into the Rapidan River. The stream changed character with the seasons. Sometimes in the autumn, it ran its full course as a murmuring brook, with mere ribbons of water gliding over the falls.

The mountain had not always been the same. About a billion years ago, the mountains of the area were relatively low, about 2,000 feet in elevation, and were devoid of plants and soil, perhaps resembling the surface of the moon. The rocks had been formed deep in the earth over a period going back another billion years, then were gradually pushed to the surface, forming the bleak, low-lying mountains.

According to geologist Thomas M. Gathright of the Virginia Division of Mineral Resources, the crests and upper slopes of the mountains were probably solid rock, while the lower slopes and valleys were spread with boulders and fragments of rocks carried down by streams. The granite rocks that formed these mountains were the same as those that are

14

now on the surface of Jones Mountain, although in the intervening time the structure and form of the mountain have drastically changed.

About 700 million years ago, extensive volcanoes spread molten lava and volcanic ash across the mountains, filling the valleys and covering all but the highest peaks. In the course of time, most of this material washed on down to the eastern plains, but surface rocks from the eruptions still cover the base of Jones Mountain in the vicinity of the Haunted Branch. Isolated remnants of the lava also remain in the Staunton River Valley, where the eroding material was caught in cracks in the granite. The nearby Hazeltop Mountain is still covered by the lava and its soil derivatives.

About 600 million years ago, the rock mountains and adjacent plains began to sink, and a sea gradually moved in from the east. Mud and sandbanks were deposited across the mountains as the beach moved west, and eventually the sea itself covered the area.

The mountains and their accumulated sediment stayed under the sea for about 250 million years. Then the water subsided as the old mountains, now considerably warped and folded, pushed again to the surface, this time much higher than they had been earlier. For the next 200 million years, erosion washed off the new deposits and wore down the high plateaus to form the ridges and hollows of the present Jones Mountain.

About one million years ago, long after the present-day structure of the mountain had formed, glacial ice pushed south nearly to the Blue Ridge Mountains, dramatically reducing temperature and causing plants of the Canadian life zone such as spruce, fir, and white birch to range south over the Appalachians. The last glaciers receded 7,000 years ago, but remnants of the Canadian forest persisted in small groves at what is now Big Meadows.

15

The Indians

Indians arrived in the Blue Ridge Mountains about 10,000 B.C. In those years, the mountains were covered with snow year-round, a result of the Ice Age. Spruce and pine forests grew on the upper slopes, but extensive grasslands and occasional groves of pine trees covered the valleys. Reindeer, buffalo, camels, and nine-foot-high mastadons and mammoths browsed the meadows.

The Indians were generally nomadic, staying at base camps while they hunted game and foraged for grapes, berries, and other plant foods. They worked the middle slopes of the mountains during the spring and summer and camped in the valleys in the winter, usually on sunny slopes near water. Not all of the Indians were nomadic, however. On the west side of the Blue Ridge Mountains, one village with about twenty huts and a population of about a hundred people was occupied continuously for 2,000 years beginning about 10,000 B.C.

The end of the northern glacial epoch around 5000 B.C. caused dramatic changes in the climate, plant cover, and wildlife of the Jones Mountain area. With the warming temperatures, oak and other hardwoods began to mix with the pines on the mountains. Scrub growth appeared in the low areas, giving the valleys the appearance of savannas. By the year 2500 B.C., mature hardwood forests were established throughout the area, and giant hemlocks thrived in the upper Staunton River Valley. But of the large game animals, only the buffalo and elk remained. Deer moved into the area, coming up from the southern lowlands.

With the coming of the hardwoods, the Indians added nuts and acorns to their diet. They also began burning openings in the forests to improve browse for game animals and drive elk and deer into hunting areas. The burned meadows were common wherever the land was flat, including Big Meadows and comparable areas in the valleys.

The Indians advanced technologically. About 1000 B.C., they began making pottery from clay. They also farmed the land, girdling trees to kill them and create clearings where they grew beans, squash, corn, and pumpkins. They fished the streams with bone hooks and sometimes used nets. The Indians migrated north and south on well-worn trails and feeder paths in the Shenandoah Valley, the Piedmont hills, and the Blue Ridge Mountains.

In the later centuries, most of the Indians seemed to prefer life in small communities where families lived in primitive huts covered with bark or mats. During this period, and up to the arrival of the Europeans, the mountain Indians were organized into small, widely scattered tribes,

Six-inch-long spear point, one of many found in the fields around Jones Mountain. Two Indian work sites have been located in the area, where the Indians chipped stone into spear points and arrow heads.

Indians camped near this site in the Rapidan Valley. Part of Jones Mountain looms in background.

each with about a hundred members. The tribes were part of a northern Virginia confederation known as the Manahoec Indians. Disputes within each tribe were settled by a council consisting of a chief and several advisors. Succession to the position of chief was by lineal descent.

The Manahoec Indians were sensitive, deeply religious people. Priests were guardians of small temples. The Indians believed in a benevolent God and worshipped the sun and natural forces such as thunder and lightning. They did not have a regular day of worship but gathered for ceremonies and feasts on special or unusual occasions such as harvest time, the end of a hunting season, or at times of fear and distress.

The Indians often engaged in sports activities and games. In the evenings around campfires, they sometimes danced and sang, keeping tempo by the rattle of gourds. The low rumble of big drums was usually a sign of restlessness and preparation for battle.

Evidence indicates that Indians regularly camped at two sites about a mile apart at the base of Jones Mountain. They hunted extensively in the area on a network of traces and trails. Work sites where they chipped white flint into spear points have been located, but archaeological excavations have not been undertaken to determine the time or duration of occupancy or whether dwellings were built.

Within a hundred years of the arrival of the English at Jamestown, the Indians of Virginia were broken and vanquished, their numbers depleted from about 18,000 to 2,000, victims of British guns, smallpox, other introduced diseases, and internal wars. In the 1620s and '30s, the English slaughtered the Powhatan tribes of the tidewater plains, avenging earlier Indian ambushes of colonial villages. But the demise of the Manahoec tribes came unexpectedly before the British penetrated the hinterlands. About 1655, the Iroquois and Susquehanna Indians of Pennsylvania, blood enemies of the Manehoecs, swarmed into Virginia, driving most of the Manahoec tribes south to the Roanoke River. There the Manahoecs as well as the northern invaders were eventually subdued by the approaching British.

Apparently, many of the isolated Blue Ridge Indians were bypassed by the northern invaders. Most of these remaining Indians pulled out of the Blue Ridge Mountains in the 1720s and '30s after the arrival of the frontiersmen. Several scattered Indian families remained in the mountain area, some "doing a great deal of mischief by firing the woods," one pioneer reported. Eventually, they intermarried with the new settlers.

Time had run out on the Indians, who had been stewards of the Blue Ridge Mountains for 12,000 years.

18

The Stanton Family

The vanguard of the frontiersmen—English and a few Scotch-Irish—ranged across the bottom lands in the early 1700s and pushed into the Great Mountains. They settled in the old Indian fields along the upper banks of streams. One of the first settlements in the area went up near a stream called Elk Run, an offshoot of the Rapidan about five miles from Jones Mountain. There, John Eddins and a few followers lived in the 1720s on "a parcel of . . . woodland ground . . . near the upper side of an old field," according to the description in the land patent.

Coming in the wake of the first trailblazers were the Cavaliers of the plantation society, gentlemen and planters, men of moderate wealth and influence who turned the borderlands of wilderness into producing farms. On May 30, 1726, planter Thomas Stanton took title to a thousand acres of frontier land on the Rapidan River, not far from the present-day Graves Mill.

Tom Stanton was not the typical Cavalier. Born about 1690, he grew up without an extensive education. He was a self-made man who had the vision to succeed. He and his wife Sarah had first arrived in the Blue Ridge area in January of 1717, when they staked out 214 acres of valley land farther down the river than their later acquisition, adjacent to a large tract owned by Virginia Governor Spotswood.

After acquiring the thousand-acre parcel in 1726, Tom Stanton and his sons Tom, Jr., and William built and operated a grist mill on the Rapidan River about four miles from Jones Mountain. With the help of slaves and indentured employees, the Stantons cleared part of the valley above the mill and opened grazing land for cattle and horses. They cultivated the bottoms and planted wheat, barley, corn, beans, and some tobacco. They also started an apple orchard, brought in sheep, and expanded their cattle herd.

Prospects for the future were good, and in 1731 Tom Stanton bought another 400 acres, paying to the Virginia land office a price of forty shillings. The new land was closer to what is now Graves Mill, located on both sides of the Rapidan. This acquisition and land owned by the sons brought the Stanton holdings to nearly 3,000 acres. The slaves lived in quarters located on the plantation. The Stanton's employees lived in houses on the vast outlying lands. Tom and Sarah and their five daughters—Frances, Sarah, Mary, Jean, and Elizabeth—lived in a manor house near the mill, a short distance from the present-day Route 662.

Within a few years, Tom Stanton built the valley into a working plantation. He often made rounds on horseback, wearing leather trousers and a long linen jacket. By the late 1730s, he had more than forty cattle, about seventy hogs, sixty-five sheep, and several horses. He did not have wagons or carts because the roads were not wide enough. Everything was transported by pack horses.

Tom Stanton garnered the harvest. One winter, he stored thirteen bushels of beans, fifty-six bushels of corn, and eighteen bushels of barley. He also had 270 gallons of cider, thirty gallons of vinegar, and eight bushels of salt.

Tom's wife Sarah ran the household and supervised the daughters. The oldest daughter, Frances, caught the eye of neighbor John Dulaney, whom she married about the year 1730. The younger girls were still in the home, growing up during the first twenty years after the Stantons settled.

Tom Stanton's vision of fulfillment was only partly realized when, still in the zenith of life, he contracted an illness beyond the cure of pioneer medicine. Soon thereafter, "being now sick and weak," he executed his last will and testament. He died when the leaves were falling in the autumn of the year 1741.

In his will, Tom Stanton entrusted to his son William the grist mill, the manor house, and the central plantation. He also gave William 200 acres of land on the north side of the river and six slaves—Adam, Judy, Sam, Winnie, Ned, and Will. To each of his daughters he bequeathed 200 acres of land. To his daughter Frances Dulaney (the name was then spelled Delaney) he also gave a "mulatto Harry and also my seal skin trunk." Son Tom Stanton, Jr., received only two items, both mentioned in the same sentence: "my still ... and also the large Bible."

In December 1741, the Court of Orange County (of which Madison County was then a part) ordered that the widow Sarah Stanton should receive "two Negro men named Ned and Old Harry," some sixty items of personal property including livestock, and an annual stipend of six pounds "current money" in recognition of her right of dower to the manor and the plantation. The order was recommended by attorney Henry Field, who was a friend of the Stantons.

Tom Stanton's remaining personal estate was sold at two public auctions held in December of 1741. Included in a lengthy list of items were money scales, candlewicks, an egg slicer, a breastplate, spinning wheels, fine linen, silk, mohair, a powdering table, furniture, shoes and boots, jackets and coats, farm implements, saddles, tanned leather, and about 225 head of livestock. Also sold were a set of carpentry tools and several stacks of lumber, the last vestiges of Tom Stanton's dreams.

Son Tom Stanton, Jr., was already an established planter who in 1728 had acquired a thousand acres of land "lying at the Great Mountains" on the north side of the Rapidan River. Tom, Jr., was active in business affairs, buying and selling and helping friends draw up legal documents. Evidence suggests that he was also a worldly man who enjoyed all the pleasures of life.

Tom, Jr., and William carried on the operation of the Stanton plantations and the grist mill. As the years passed, the businesses prospered, at least by Cavalier standards. William increased his land holdings and eventually acquired twenty-nine slaves and a substantial increase in his tax assessment. Tom's fortune was such that by 1749 he was able to give his infant son, as a present, one Negro man. Eventually, the Stantons moved away, passing from the scene of Jones Mountain, but the progeny of the patriarch Tom Stanton, Sr., would continue for several generations through the lineage of his daughter Frances Dulaney.

Other Early Settlers

While the Stanton's were still building, other settlers arrived in the area. In 1727, Thomas Jackson acquired a large tract of land on the north side of the Rapidan River "by a rock of stone." John Bush purchased land about 1735, establishing a family name that would be prominent in the mountain area for a hundred years. In 1736, John and Mary Garth acquired a large parcel on a stream known today as Garth (pronounced "Gath") Run, flowing from the upper reaches of Bluff Mountain. Also settling on adjacent lands were Francis Kirtley, George Simmons, and Francis Conway. Conway purchased 10,000 acres of land on the river that now bears his name.

The first land patents on Jones Mountain were granted to pioneers John Pickitt and Jeremiah Bryan. Pickitt acquired about 250 acres in 1737. About half of the land was in what is now Shenandoah National Park, along the banks of the Rapidan and the lower Staunton River. Pickitt's land included part of the present-day Staunton River Trail, from the trailhead to the first big cascades of the river. From the river, the parcel extended up to the ridges of Jones Mountain. John Pickitt apparently lived there about five years, then moved on.

About this time, Jeremiah Bryan purchased land in what is today the Staunton River Valley of Shenandoah Park. His land was also on the present-day Staunton River Trail, below Bear Church Rock, and extended across both sides of the river. Although Bryan was one of the first small landowners in the back country of Jones Mountain, it is doubtful that he lived there. He also owned valley land in the Rapidan area, where

21

his heirs lived after he died. Some of the heirs lived on the Staunton tract in later years.

Bryan's mountain place came close to a 40,000-acre parcel, known later as the Big Survey, which was owned then by Thomas Smith. Part of the Big Survey extended into the Staunton River valley below Fork Mountain. In the valleys and hollows a few miles to the north, the Big Survey was heavily encroached by squatters, a situation that seldom developed on Jones Mountain, which was buffered by plantations.

The present-day Graves Mill Fire Road (on the Rapidan River) undoubtedly dates to the 1730s. The original Staunton River Trail probably was opened in the mid-1740s. Both routes were originally narrow pack horse "roads" (as they were called then) about three feet wide. Indian occupation in the vicinity suggests that both trails were originally Indian traces.

Land boundaries, early building sites, and the terrain of the lower valley indicate that the original Staunton River pack horse road followed what is now a dim trail higher on the slopes of Jones Mountain, coinciding with the present-day trail only at the great bend of the river and near the trailhead. In later decades, parts of the trail were plowed under, obliterated by clear-cuts and grazing, and dismembered by logging roads.

1979 photo of the Staunton River Trail shows part of the land that was patented to John Pickitt in 1737.

David and Elizabeth Jones

George the second by the Grace of God of Great Britain France and Ireland. King Defender of the Faith. To all to whom these presents shall come Greeting. Know ye that for diverse good Cause and Consideration but more especially for and in consideration of the importation of Two Persons to dwell within this our Colony and Dominion of Virginia whose names are David Jones and Elizabeth Jones. . . .

We have Given Granted and Confirmed and by these Presents for us our Heirs and Successors do Give Grant and Confirm unto David Jones one certain Tract or Parcel of Land containing three hundred and fifty Acres lying and being in the Parish of Saint Mark in the County of Orange and bounded as follows (to wit) Beginning at four small white Oaks and a red Oak on the South side of Stanton's River being a branch of the Rappadan River and running Thence. . . .

Yielding and Paying unto us our Heirs and Successors for every fifty Acres of Land and so proportionately for a lesser or Greater Quantity than fifty Acres the Fee Rent of one Shilling Yearly to be paid upon the Feast of Saint Michael the Arch Angel. . . .

Excerpts from land grant
Colony of Virginia
June 1, 1741

Arriving from England in 1741, David and Elizabeth Jones purchased 350 acres of land adjoining the far end of Tom Stanton's tract. The price was twenty-five shillings, payable to the colony of Virginia in four annual installments. The Jones land was more than a mile long, located on the south and west side of the Rapidan River (known then as Stanton's River) at the present-day site of Graves Mill. The back boundary extended northwesterly up the steep flank of the Great Mountain, then crossed the valley on a southerly course 7,920 feet to a hollow near the top of the present-day Kentuck Mountain.

Few facts can be reconstructed about the lives of David and Elizabeth Jones, transplants from southern England to the outposts of British America. They had at least one son, David, Jr. The cost of their transatlantic voyage was paid to a mariner in East Greenwich, Kent County, England, southeast of London. David apparently was a man of some means, since the contract for the transportation did not require a period of indentured servitude.

In the summer and fall of 1741, David and Elizabeth apparently spent much of their time poring over plans for their new land and constructing a millrace for a new grist mill. They cleared the first fields and broke some of the first trails in the shadow of the mountain that would bear their name. Neighbors probably helped them build a cabin for their home.

On December 2, 1741, a man named Jones showed up at the public auction of Thomas Stanton's estate. He was the highest bidder for two sides of tanned leather, sixteen pounds of old brass, and other items, for which he paid one pound, sixteen shillings, and eleven pence. The man may have been the newcomer David Jones, the only Jones who owned land in the immediate area in 1741.

The patent from the colonial land office required David Jones to "cultivate and improve" at least twenty-five acres of the 350-acre parcel. This was no problem, since the tract included about 200 acres of what is today rich agricultural land. In the 1740s, almost all of the land was forested, with extensive stands of chestnuts, hickories, yellow poplars, and several species of oak. Dogwood and mountain laurel flourished in the understory.

David and Elizabeth Jones took their obligations seriously. They worked the land, and it produced income. They apparently grew corn and other grains. Although tobacco was a booming business elsewhere, it is doubtful that David and Elizabeth grew this crop. There is no record that they or their neighbors owned loose tobacco or the hogsheads or wagons that were required for transporting the crop. Moreover, it would be some years before the rolling roads, used in shipping tobacco, were extended to the Great Mountains.

By 1745, David had liquidated his debt and cleared the title to his land. He acquired the colonial status of freehold farmer. In the meantime, he completed the construction of his grist mill near a fork in the river, apparently near an old Indian field.

In the few years that David and Elizabeth Jones lived in the area, they emerged with some standing, as evidenced by the landmarks that carried their name. The valley area became known for the next sixty years as Jones (or Jones's) Mill. (There was also a "Jack Jones Mill" on Thomas Jackson's land about six miles down the river.) The stream known today as Kinsey Run, which flows into the Rapidan at the present-day Graves Mill, was known then and for the next 150 years as Jones Run.

The big mountain above Jones Mill became known eventually as Jones Mountain, although early survey records generally referred to it simply as part of the Great Mountains. There is some evidence that the mountain was called Stony Mountain before the name Jones Mountain caught on. At least one deed referred to it as Stony Mountain, although the word may have been used merely to describe the terrain. A map in 1825 identified the entire mountain range as Bluff Mountain. The name Jones Mountain originally applied only to the outermost ridge closest to

Jones Mill but later embraced the entire range extending from the high tableland, past Cat Knob, ending at Laurel Gap and the Sag, several miles from Jones Mill.

Despite his successes, David Jones would never have the opportunity to expand his holdings. He and Elizabeth were scarcely established, just eight or nine years after their arrival from England, when death struck them down. Apparently, there is no written confirmation of the details of their death. According to a story, they were attacked and captured by Indians, who took them into the mountains. Their scalped bodies were found, according to the story, on the top of Jones Mountain.

County records indicate that David Jones died about 1750. On June 19, 1751, David Jones, Jr., sold the land to Thomas Rucker. Records indicate that David, Jr., left the area, settling in the more populated Piedmont hills near Orange, Virginia, where he was a planter.

Surveys of the Jones Mountain Area

Some fifteen years after the colony of Virginia granted land patents to Tom Stanton and other early settlers, a British baron challenged the colony's right to sell the land. Thomas Lord Fairfax, the sixth baron of Cameron, contended that the land, in what is now the southern part of Madison County, was part of his 5,282,000-acre Northern Neck grant, which he inherited from his mother, Catherine Culpeper Fairfax. Catherine had inherited the grant from her father Thomas, the second Lord Culpeper, a former Virginia governor-for-life until he was fired by the king for spending too much time in England. Thomas had inherited the land from his father John, the first Lord Culpeper, who got it from King Charles II as a reward for supporting King Charles I before the latter was executed during the English Civil War.

The original grant, made in 1649 and reconfirmed in 1660, described the southern boundary of the Northern Neck as running with the Rappahannock River, or, more precisely, the stream that formed the headwaters of the Rappahannock. But, since the Rappahannock had never been surveyed to its source, Lord Fairfax, in a petition to the king, argued that the main headwaters flowed from the branch known as the Rapidan, where both he and the colony had been selling land.

Survey crews were dispatched in 1736 to gather data, one crew going up the Rappahannock and the other up the Rapidan. But the Rapidan crew, under surveyor John Graham, took a left turn about five miles from Jones Mountain and ended up in the Conway River Valley below Cat Knob. The upshot of this was that the Lords of Trade in London

25

ruled that the Fairfax line should follow the Conway River at the south base of Jones Mountain, thus vesting to Lord Fairfax the proprietary rights to the mountain and the present-day Graves Mill valley.

In 1745, the King's Council ruled that all previous land grants in the disputed territory were legally valid. The effect of this decision protected the earlier grants made to the Stantons, John Pickitt, David Jones, and others in the vicinity of Jones Mountain but gave the bulk of the mountain to Lord Fairfax.

Then came one of the major surveys of history. In 1746, a field crew of thirty men under surveyor Thomas Lewis charted the Fairfax Line from the Conway River west across the Shenandoah Valley and the Allegheny Mountains. Lewis, twenty-eight, was a tall, studious man with extremely poor eyesight. Some of the men in the party were gentlemen of the Virginia aristocracy, who brought along valets. One member of the party was Joshua Fry, a former professor of mathematics at Oxford University. Another was Captian Peter Jefferson, the county surveyor in Charlottesville, who was also the father of a gifted child, three-year-old Thomas Jefferson.

Most of the Fairfax survey was outside the area of Jones Mountain, but before starting their four-month bushwhack across the valley, the group camped for several days below Cat Knob while surveying the hollows on both sides of the valley at the base of Jones Mountain, the object being to locate the main headsprings of the Conway. The going was rough in the mountain country. "Several horses [were] very much hurt amongst the Rocks on the mountain," Lewis said in his journal.

Among the areas which they surveyed was "the west fork . . . that which makes the place Calld the Divels Jump," wrote Lewis. He described the lower part of this stream as "the mouth of the Divels Dich . . . [a] Branch oposite to a Small Island on the Right . . ." Nearly 200 years later, still known as the Devils Ditch, the hollow would be the home place of mountaineer Mat Taylor. Today, the area forms the dividing line between the Shenandoah National Park and the Rapidan Wildlife Management Area.

Eventually, Lewis found a headspring in another hollow, which the commissioners of the survey agreed was the best place to begin the westward course. That point on the Fairfax Line is today in Shenandoah National Park below the Laurel Prong Trail, about a half mile from Bootens Gap. From that point, the survey gang climbed to the crest of Hazeltop Ridge, dropped down to Naked Creek, and headed northwest across the mountains and valleys.

Part of Jones Mountain was surveyed in 1737, but the first major surveys were done in the 1740s. Local resident Henry Downs surveyed the lower areas near the valley about 1742. In 1748 and 1749, George Hume surveyed the top of Jones and Fork Mountains and the present-day Staunton River Valley. George Hume was no ordinary surveyor. The son of a Scottish lord, he was imprisoned and later banished from his homeland for participating in a political rebellion in 1715. Hume migrated to British America, where he worked as a surveyor and served as an officer in the British colonial army. One of his surveying assistants, whom he trained, was young George Washington. Hume later worked for Lord Fairfax from 1743 to 1750, when he became the foremost authority on Jones Mountain and other areas in that part of the Fairfax territory. Later, George Hume was commissioned as county surveyor, replacing his former student George Washington, who had held the post for two years.

The Mid-1700s

With the establishment of Jones Mill and settlement within earshot of the Great Mountains, the pioneers opened a narrow cart trail about four feet wide from near Elk Run to Jones Mill, following about the same route as the present-day Route 662 from Wolftown to Graves Mill. The route apparently was blazed by notches on trees, as was the custom. The local people called it Stanton's Road and used it mostly for pack horse traffic. The route meandered to the river to provide watering stops for the horses and oxen.

The Rapidan River was first known as Stanton's River. The lower part of the stream, below the juncture with the Conway, was known as the Rappadan (pronounced and later spelled Rapid Ann), named about 1713 by Governor Spotswood in honor of Queen Anne of Great Britain. The upper branches of the river, known today as the Rapidan and the Staunton, were known in the 1700s and early 1800s as the North and South Forks (or Prongs or Branches) of the Stanton River (later spelled Staunton but always pronounced "Stan-ten"). The mountain known to-day as Fork Mountain was known then by the same name, although sometimes it was called Forked Mountain. To the early settlers, the pointed summits resembled the prongs of a fork.

The high rock formation above the South Prong of the Stanton River, known today as Bear Church Rock, was known then and for the next 150 years as the Rock Church, apparently so named because of the temple-like form of the cliffs that stood against the horizon when viewed from the first cleared fields of the valley. The backbone ridge behind the

Survey description and plat, dated August 30, 1748, signed by George Hume, for a tract of land on the Staunton River below Bear Church Rock. Richard Durret purchased the land from Lord Fairfax in 1749. (The land is today in Shenandoah National Park.)

Rock Church, connecting with the main body of Jones Mountain, was commonly called Church Mountain, or sometimes Rock Church Mountain.

With the first trails broken, more settlers pushed toward the Great Mountains in the 1740s. In 1749, Richard Durret acquired a tract of land on both sides of the South Prong below the Rock Church. Durret apparently cleared the extensive slopes above the present-day Staunton River Trail and constructed the first cabin on the back side of Jones Mountain. The site would later be known as Bush Field. The original pack horse road passed through the area. (The location of a large cemetery on this tract is one of the telltales of its earliest occupation. The land today is about two miles inside Shenandoah National Park.)

By the 1750s, the English were pushing on across the Great Mountains, joining the Scotch-Irish and Germans of the Shenandoah Valley in the westward transmigration. Fierce Indian attacks on the western settlers erupted into the French and Indian War, in which Virginia colonial troops fought under Colonel George Washington. The British government in London, concerned about the continuing confrontations with Indians, tried by legislation in 1763 to halt further westward settlement. But the young colonial pioneers, a large part of whom were born on the American continent, resented the king's intrusion and ignored the order.

Stirred by a restless spirit, the American frontiersmen poured on across the mountains toward the land of promise. By the second half of the 18th century, some of the original settlers near Jones Mountain moved on with the westward tide and other pioneers streamed into the lush Jones Mill Valley to build homes and plant new crops.

Roads were improved so that pack horses could move deeper into the valleys and up the hollows of the Great Mountains. A road was built across the outlying mountains to the German and English farms on the Robertson River, and Tom Stanton's road to Jones Mill was widened and improved for wagon traffic.

The improvement of Stanton's Road brought a dramatic change to the economy of the valley. Farmers, no longer boxed in by narrow roads, began shipping produce to coastal markets. The biggest money crop was tobacco, which they hauled out by ox-cart, wagon, and in hogsheads. Plantations expanded, and new planters moved into the valley.

Zachary Lewis and Isaac Smith

The early land grants in the area often went to investors who sometimes held the land or subdivided and sold to new settlers or former indentured servants who had served out their contracts. Two of the most ambitious and successful speculators were Isaac Smith and Zachary Lewis, who monopolized the land grants on Jones Mountain. Isaac Smith started in July of 1740 with a modest purchase of 200 acres of valley farmland near the Stanton Mill, which he acquired from Tom Stanton, paying in annual installments at the Feast of Saint Michael. Then in 1742, he bought John Pickitt's land at the branches of the Stanton River, where the present-day Staunton feeds into the Rapidan. The parcel extended across Jones Mountain, where it adjoined David Jones' land.

Ten years later, in 1752 and 1753, Isaac Smith launched headlong into land acquisition, buying up nine more parcels totaling 2,918 acres. Part of the land ranged up the South Fork to near the top of Jones Mountain. One parcel was located "on Garth's Spring Nigh the head of the South Branch of Stanton River . . . on the side of a Mountain . . . Stony Mountain." The area is today the hollow of Garth Spring Run in the Shenandoah National Park, where an ancient abandoned trail climbs a rocky course to the top of the mountain.

In January of 1752, Smith bought valley land near Jones Mill. One tract was adjacent to the lands of "David Jones dec'd and Robert Key and Thomas Stanton dec'd," extending up a mountain "to a Poor Ridge."

In the years 1753 to 1756, Zachary Lewis (he signed it John Z.) bought nearly 1,700 acres extending along the top of Jones Mountain, down into the hollows, and across Fork Mountain. On January 10, 1755, he acquired the land that is now the site of the Jones Mountain Cabin. Zachary's other holdings included the tableland (part of which was later known as Garth Spring Field) and the lower part of the South Fork (Staunton River) Valley adjacent to Isaac Smith's tracts. Most of Lewis' land is today in Shenandoah National Park.

The deed descriptions of Garth Spring and the tableland were written by George Hume about 1748 after he surveyed the top of Jones (or Stony) Mountain. Apparently, the Garths or their descendants grazed cattle on the mountain-top flat above the spring. The use of this remote area during the early days of the frontier suggests that the tableland may have been an old Indian field before 1730.

The vast forested lands of Isaac Smith and Zachary Lewis buffered the small inholdings of Richard Durret (and later Mark Stower), shutting out further settlement in the Jones Mountain area for several years. (Apparently, however, there had been some occupation of Lewis' land before he bought it, when it was in the domain of Lord Fairfax back in the 1740s. A man named Gilgo, probably a squatter, apparently settled at the headspring of a side stream off the present-day Staunton River, and someone named Wilson apparently lived near the mouth of that stream. When surveyor George Hume scouted and charted the hollow in 1748, he identified Wilson Run and located Gilgo Spring at the headwaters. Neither Gilgo nor Wilson was a landowner or taxpayer of record.)

The Graves Family

In May of the year 1760, a young planter named Thomas Graves crossed the mountain country from the lower Conway River and made his first land purchase in the valley of Stanton's River. He was already a man of resources, owning a thousand acres of land on the Conway River and Garth Run, which he inherited from early Graves settlers. When he was nineteen, some eight years before his arrival in the Stanton Valley, Tom had married pretty Sarah Dulaney, a woman of good pedigree, being the daughter of Frances Stanton Dulaney and the granddaughter of the original settler and planter Tom Stanton. At the wedding, Tom Graves was attired in the style of a colonial gentleman, complete with silk hose and knee breeches. He probably also wore a massive silver buckle, as was his custom, because Tom Graves had a proud and aristocratic quality—descriptive words found in the diary of his own granddaughter.

Tom had every right to be proud, since he traced his lineage all the way back to the origins of British America. He was the fourth-generation descendant of Captain Thomas Graves, who settled in Jamestown in 1608, arriving from England on the ship *Mary and Margaret*. The captain's son was Francis, whose son was Thomas (of Essex County), whose son was John (of Spotsylvania County), whose son was Tom Graves, the proud husband of Sarah Dulaney.

Such was the man who settled near Jones Mill on a flat above the river about 500 feet from the east slope of Jones Mountain. In the years that followed, Tom Graves expanded his estate until he owned about 3,000 acres. His principal acquisitions came in 1784, when he purchased several of Zachary Lewis' holdings on and around Jones Mountain, including the site of the present-day Jones Mountain Cabin. He also acquired most of the fertile valley land in the vicinity of Jones Mill. By purchasing these lands, Tom Graves effectively continued the buffer against development and subdivision of most of the outlying mountain area.

31

Graves turned his valley estate into a vast tobacco plantation, which he supervised from the central manor above the river. (The building was destroyed by fire in 1938.) Here, Tom and Sarah also reared four sons and eleven daughters, the last nine children being daughters. The oldest child was Susannah, born in 1758, before the Graves bought land in the Stanton valley. The youngest, Liza, was born twenty-nine years later, in 1787.

For fifty years, Tom Graves' main activity was managing his farms. His staple crops were tobacco and apples, but he also grew wheat, hemp, and several varieties of corn. The apples were used for the production of brandy, for which he had a storage capacity of at least 650 gallons. He also stored about 400 pounds of milled hemp and sixty barrels of flour. At one point, he had eighteen hogsheads of tobacco valued at nearly 300 pounds (Virginia currency). Livestock included about forty hogs, a small herd of cattle, and a flock of sheep. It is likely that the cattle grazed during the summer at Garth Spring on the tableland of Jones Mountain, where native bluegrass thrived. Tom Graves purchased the tract in the 1780s.

As the Graves family grew, so did Sarah Graves' responsibility for supervising the manor. Her kitchen and furnishings were not elaborate

Tom Graves' manor house near Graves Mill, headquarters of 3,000-acre plantation from 1780s to 1810. The building was destroyed by fire in 1938.

32

but they were adequate. Most of the furniture was made of walnut. Some of it was pine. Sarah had a wooden clock and a large looking glass. The spacious kitchen was equipped for a large family—forty earthen plates, eighty-four pewter plates, a case of knives and forks, twelve tea kettles, seven iron pots.... The family also had three spinning wheels.

Graves had a large blacksmith shop, the site of which is now marked by dark soil in a cultivated field. Here, his blacksmith repaired and maintained a wagon, a road coach, several plows, and other farm implements. He apparently also worked leather and made shoes.

At the height of the plantation operations, Tom Graves and his oldest children owned upwards of fifty slaves. Most of them were quartered on Jones Run, where a small slave church was located. A slave cemetery marked with fieldstones was located in what is now Kinsey Hollow on the south side of Jones Mountain. The slaves were assigned as field hands on the plantation and house servants at the manor. All of them addressed Sarah Dulaney Graves as "My Lady." Records indicate that Tom Graves traded in the African slave market, since he owned at least two women of recent African origin who, according to a diary account, were easily frightened.

Tom Graves enjoyed leisure and the good life of a planter. He had two stills, one of which was probably for personal use. He enjoyed sipping wine, decanted and served to him from tumblers. He probably

The site of the manor house on the Graves plantation today.

33

Water wheel at Graves Mill, built in 1799. The earlier Jones Mill was located on the same site. Grinding wheel inside was made of wood. Mill ceased operation in 1940s.

A 1981 view of the Graves Mill water wheel.

drank brandy from the plantation's commercial stock. He had a desk and a bookcase, both made of black walnut. Like other men of class, Tom owned a set of surveying instruments and a measuring chain. He hunted wild game, using one of his two shotguns. His livery was well equipped for trail riding. He apparently rode often to visit neighbors, including some with whom he had business accounts—among them John Booten, David Snyder, Jeremiah Jarrell, Angus Rucker, and John Eddins. Occasionally, Tom and Sarah visited William and Tom Stanton, Jr., both of whom were getting along in years.

The Graves spent part of their time reading. Included in their small library were law books, a physician's manual, a history text, *Guthries Grammar*, *Pilgrim's Progress*, a large miscellaneous collection, and several almanacs.

Tom and Sarah Graves were among the thousands of Virginians who broke from the traditional Episcopal Church of England, during the decline of British influence, and became active Baptists. In their home they had a prayer book, several religious faith books, and two Bibles, one of which was the Graves family Bible. In 1773, Tom helped organize the Rapid Ann Baptist Meetinghouse at a settlement known today as Wolftown. The church started with thirty-seven charter members, some of whom were from Jones Mill.

Tom Graves was also active in the community and emerged as a leading citizen of the mountain area. He helped organize the new Madison County courthouse when the new county was split off from Culpeper County in 1793. Also that year, Graves was appointed justice of the peace. In later years, he was addressed as Captain Graves.

In 1799, Graves constructed a water-powered grist mill beside the Stanton (now Rapidan) River, which he operated under the name of Thomas Graves and Sons. The new mill was on the site of the original Jones Mill. The family also operated a saw mill at the site.

Thereafter, the valley community of Jones Mill became known as Graves Mill. The Stanton Road took on the name Graves Road. About the same time, the name of the Great Mountains changed to the Blue Ridge Mountains, a name that had been used increasingly for several years. And after the Revolution, the colony of Virginia became the state of Virginia. General George Washington had become the national hero—and one who drew local attention when he passed near Jones Mountain on October 1, 1784, stopping his servants and pack horses seven miles from Graves Mill, where he spent the night at the Early house.

Meanwhile, the spelling of the Stanton River changed to Staunton, apparently in deference to the spelling used in identifying the city of Staunton in the Shenandoah Valley. That city was named in honor of Lady Gooch, a Staunton, who was the wife of Governor William Gooch. The city was founded by John Lewis, who received the land as a grant from Governor Gooch. It was John Lewis' son Thomas who had supervised the Fairfax survey at the base of Jones Mountain in 1746. Thomas Lewis and his associates Joshua Fry and Peter Jefferson later produced a map that identified the river by the spelling "Staunton." Peter's son Thomas Jefferson used the same spelling in 1784, when he prepared a map of Virginia as a supplement to his classic work, *Notes on the State of Virginia.*

The modified spelling was seldom used by local surveyors, who traced their spelling to the original deeds of Tom Stanton and other early settlers. A county map in 1791 identified the stream as "Stanton River." In the years after 1800, when the Stantons were gone, the surveyors slowly yielded to the new spelling. The pronunciation ("Stan-ten") remained the same.

During the period 1800 to 1880, the prefixes South and North Forks (of the Staunton River) gradually phased out, giving way, respectively, to Staunton River and Rapid Ann River. As the change evolved, the South Fork was occasionally called the South Fork of the Rapid Ann.

Tom Graves was, above all, a devoted family man. His sons not only became partners in the mill business but also were permitted to stake out their own homesteads on the Graves plantation. At least three of the sons took land on or adjacent to Jones Mountain. Benjamin Graves occupied part of the broad Jones Run Hollow (now Kinsey Hollow). His back lines extended to the ridge of Church Mountain and included part of what is now the Jones Mountain Trail. (The tract later went to Benjamin's son-in-law Charles Yancey.)

Son John Graves settled on low land near the east slope of the mountain. Asa Graves took a parcel of land on the east side of the Rapid Ann River across from the Graves manor. Asa built and expanded his plantation until he owned over 2,500 acres. Eventually, he inherited the grist mill and the saw mill. Today, Asa's home and the old mill are the only surviving relics of the bygone era. (Descendants of John Graves now own and operate the famous Graves Mountain Lodge near Syria, Virginia.

John's son Paschal moved across the Blue Ridge to Page County, where the latter's son James Madison Graves was born. James' son Robert Alexander Graves settled at Syria. Robert's son was Elvin, the father of Jimmy Graves, who in 1981 was the proprietor of the Graves Mountain Lodge. Jimmy is a sixth-generation descendant of Tom Graves and a tenth-generation descendant of Captain Thomas Graves of Jamestown.)

Tom Graves also looked out for his daughters. He was especially proud on December 22, 1795, when he gave the hand of his daughter Lydia, twenty, in marriage to young Joel Eddins, a native son, descendant of the first Elk Run settlers. Presiding at the wedding was Rev. George Eve, a man of stature who was a friend and confidant of James Madison, the future president.

The Eddins Family

Joel and Lydia Eddins selected a parcel of 267 acres (which Tom Graves later deeded to them) across the east side of Jones Mountain, the same parcel that John Pickitt had acquired in 1737 and Isaac Smith had bought in 1742. The land lay at the head of the long Graves Mill Valley and included what is today the lower Staunton River Trail. The tract included both sides of what is now the Rapidan River. The mountain land was rough and broken, but the lower slopes, most of which were probably already cleared, would make good crop land, rich and fertile.

On the east side of the stream, within hearing range of the rapids, Joel and Lydia found a place below a spring for their home. Mountains rose on three sides. The site, now in Shenandoah National Park, was back from what is now called the Big Bridge, marked today by a stone abutment. (The stone work was constructed in the 1890s. The bridge washed out in 1942.) Not far downstream from the bridge was Indian Rock, a large boulder with a circular depression on top believed by the early settlers to be a former grinding stone used by Indians. The site was not far from a probable prehistoric Indian camp. (A rampaging flood in 1893 washed the boulder downstream about fifty yards, where the rock came to rest with the depression on the side.)

In 1797, Lydia bore her husband a daughter, whom they named Clarissa, the granddaughter of Tom Graves and great-great-granddaughter of Tom Stanton. In the years that followed, Joel Eddins turned his attention to the details of transforming the strung-out mountain slopes into a profitable plantation. He had plenty of help. Several slaves removed the loose rocks from the soil and stacked them in piles. They planted tobacco, rye, and hemp. On slopes too rocky to till, they set out apple trees. And within a few years, Joel Eddins settled down to the life of a successful planter.

37

In April of 1808, Joel acquired more land, an adjoining tract extending up the Stanton River (or South Fork) and across Jones Mountain. The parcel included the Jones Mountain Cabin site and the Rock Church. Joel purchased the land from his brother Abraham, who had received it as a gift from Tom Graves when Abraham married Grave's daughter Polly. This acquisition brought Joel's holdings on Jones Mountain to nearly a thousand acres, including the first mile and a half of the present-day Staunton River Trail. He turned the lower slopes into grazing land for sheep and cattle and expanded his orchards and grain fields.

Joel Eddins owned three horses whom he called Dick, Jim and George—Jim being a mare. They were trained for both harness and saddle. The slaves used them to plow the fields for planting. Joel rode the horses and used them for packing supplies.

After the river roads were widened and graded, wagons were used to haul in supplies and carry out produce, principally tobacco and hemp. Joel also shipped apple brandy, which he fermented and distilled in commercial quantities in eleven brandy barrels.

Joel and Lydia Eddins lived comfortably at the Big Bridge. At night, the house was lighted by candles and at least one lamp. Joel sat at a desk while he went over his accounts and conducted business. The Eddins had adequate food and good wine. Joel owned twice the number of decanters and tumblers that his father-in-law, Tom Graves, owned. Joel and Lydia also enjoyed coffee, which they ground in their own coffee mill. Their furniture was walnut. They had several chests, tables (including walnut folding tables), cupboards, and trunks. Lydia had ten tablecloths. Their bed coverings were made of double-woven material, products of their own spinning wheels.

But the Staunton River plantation lacked the aristocratic air that pervaded the Graves plantation. The Eddins home was much smaller than the Graves manor. Joel Eddins' personal estate was impressive, but his accounts were heaviest on agricultural yields and devoid of such luxuries as road coaches and serving trays.

Planter Tom Graves died in 1810. He was probably buried in the Graves family cemetery near the central manor, enclosed today by a low rock wall. In his will he bequeathed to his daughter Lydia 100 pounds (Virginia currency). Tom Graves' total personal estate was appraised at 3,000 pounds. It was about enough money to furnish thirty plantation homes or buy 750 head of good cattle. In addition to the personal estate, he still owned the manor, the mill, and about 600 acres of real estate, having already given 80 percent of his land to his children.

The Bush Family

When she was eighteen, Clarissa Eddins was seen often in the company of young Willis Bush, whose family lived on the Rapid Ann north of the Eddins tract. Willis' father and mother, Joshua and Frances Bush, had settled there in the spring of 1794 on a flat below the east slope of Fork Mountain. There, the Bushes reared five children: Elizabeth, William, Caleb, Willis, and Abram. Joshua Bush and Joel Eddins were trusted friends, and the two families often visited.

During the months of their courtship, Clarissa Eddins and Willis Bush probably ventured often up the valley road of the Staunton River, where the fields of the plantation sloped gently from Jones Mountain. On a slight rise a mile up the river, they could command a view of the valley with the long, narrow fields to the right and the steep, rugged slopes of Fork Mountain to the left. They must have liked what they saw, because after they were married, on December 18, 1815, it was in this part of the Staunton River valley that they made their home.

Willis Bush and his father-in-law Joel Eddins climbed Jones Mountain and staked out a parcel of 265 acres for Willis and his new wife. The land was at the west end of the Eddins plantation, extending downstream along the great bend of the river, then up and across the ridge of Church Mountain, back by the Rock Church and down again to the river. The boundaries meandered in the fashion of early surveys, changing course sixteen times. The deed described landmarks and the precise metes and bounds, as was the custom in all of the early surveys of Jones Mountain.

Fieldstones in the Graves family cemetery near the plantation manor.

In acquiring this parcel, Willis and Clarissa Bush became the tenth owners of the site of the Jones Mountain Cabin. The deed described the lower fields on the Staunton River but made no reference to any clearings or settlements on the mountain below the Rock Church.

Evidence suggests that the Staunton River Road was constructed about this time, laid out about as it is today, replacing the earlier pack horse path. A stone retaining wall lined most of the road along the first two miles of its route. Slaves undoubtedly did the original road work. In later years, the county government graded the route and relocated parts of the road. (Almost all of the retaining walls were removed in 1943.)

Willis and Clarissa Bush probably settled on a flat just above the retaining wall, marked today by a high bank above the Staunton River Trail. The open field extended back about a thousand feet from the river. Years later, the site would be occupied by Dave (Fat) Breeden.

The Bushes were not alone in the Staunton River Valley. Other landowners upstream included Franky Branner, Adam Willard, George Baily, and William and Elizabeth Taylor. Branner, one of the legatees of Jeremiah Bryan, bought up most of the interests of the other heirs in 1804 and acquired two additional tracts on both sides of the river. The Bryan land had probably been occupied off and on since the 1750s. During that period, the legatees of Jeremiah Bryan (including Mark Stowers and later

Site of the old Lillard place on the Staunton River Trail. The land was settled by newlyweds Willis and Clarissa Bush in 1815. Earlier, it was part of the Joel Eddins plantation. The land was first patented by Zachary Lewis in 1755.

William Stowers) used the land across the river from the Rock Church. They probably lived there.

Also in the valley were several slaves, including two or three whom Willis Bush inherited from his father Joshua, who died in 1814. In the 1820s, Joel Eddins owned eleven slaves who worked in both the Staunton and Rapidan Valleys. Their names were Tom, Joe, Feby, Fanny, Ann, Mary, Evy, Lewis, Frank, Reuben, and Sarah.

Another slave owner was Caleb Bush (a brother of Willis), who in 1822 purchased the next parcel upstream from Willis on the Jones Mountain side of the river. The ninety-acre tract was part of the original Richard Durret patent. The land included a gently sloping sixty-acre meadow on the Staunton River, downstream from where the present-day Jones Mountain Trail begins. Oldtimers even today refer to this area as Bush Field, although it is now deeply forested (part of the national park), and the oldtimers have no recollection of anyone named Bush living in the area. (Six generations of the Bush family lived in the Jones Mountain area from the 1730s to about 1840.) What the oldtimers do know is that a cabin stood on the site, crumbing into the earth in the 1890s.

Caleb Bush's log cabin (which probably was occupied earlier by Franky Branner) was upstream from the mouth of a hollow near the west end of the field. A wagon road led to the site. A cemetery with field-rock headstones, known in later years as the Bush Field cemetery (sometimes called the Jenkins cemetery) was near the west end of the field. Located on the original patent land, the cemetery probably goes back to the colonial period.

It was probably during the 1820s, when the Bush brothers owned Bush Field as well as the top of the mountain, that a switchback trail was constructed from the lower slopes up to the flat above the future site of the Jones Mountain Cabin. Caleb or Willis probably used the trail as a stock path for cattle, which may have grazed the flat and the mountain slopes during the summer months. It was a common practice in those years for farmers to take their cattle to high ground near springs during the summer, where flies and other insects were less bothersome.

The longer route to the flat, following the lower part of the present-day Jones Mountain Trail, probably was not constructed until the 1840s, when wagons were in greater use in the mountains. The road may have been a stock path in earlier years, when Tom Graves owned most of the land.

The Bush and Eddins families were shaken by tragedy in 1828, when they heard the news of the death of Joel Eddins. Joel's body was reportedly found weighted down by a large rock, tied to his neck by a rope, in a deep pool of the Rapidan River below Indian Rock. Ill-wind had apparently blown his way, and the death was attributed to suicide!

Willis and Clarissa Bush did not remain long in the Staunton River Valley. They sold their land to John H. Graves and left with their children about 1830. The children were the sixth generation of the pedigree of Tom Stanton.

New Settlers, 1825-1850

During the second quarter of the nineteenth century, most of the land on Jones Mountain was bought by local investors seeking to turn a business profit. After 1820, land values went up from $2 an acre to $5. The speculators were schooled in the art of cash flow, buying and selling and sometimes subdividing at a clip almost too fast to reconstruct. To compound matters, some of their buying and selling was to one another.

When the dust had settled, the old-line families were gone from Jones Mountain and the Staunton River valley. John H. Graves, who had bought the cabin tract from Willis Bush, sold in 1836 to Acrey B. Jones, a newcomer who was, himself, lured by the prospects of land investment.

Acrey, the son of county resident John Jones, married Nancy Powell in 1825 and brought his bride to the valley of the Rapid Ann below Fork Mountain. In the next twenty years, Acrey bought about ten more parcels of land totaling nearly 1,500 acres. He then sold or leased most of the land, including the site of the Jones Mountain Cabin. That parcel went to Philander Goodall, who thereupon became the thirteenth owner of the land since 1660. And like the other twelve, Goodall lived elsewhere.

Philander Goodall's record was one for the book. Born in 1794, he arrived in the area shortly after 1817, when he married Mourning Marshall. The couple first settled on a flat above the Rapid Ann about a quarter mile downstream from the present-day Hoover Road. There, Philander made his start with two apple trees and some seed for orchard grass. He acquired some level ground, cultivated the soil, and produced good crops. Philander had a good head for business. He saved his money, bought more land, and sold at a good profit.

In later years, Philander Goodall acquired several other parcels of land, including the cabin tract and large holdings on the Staunton River Road. Eventually, the Goodalls moved downstream to a tract on the present-day national park boundary, known for the next century as the Goodall Farm. Here, Philander and Mourning reared twelve children, two of whom they named Benjamin Franklin and Thomas Jefferson.

Mourning Goodall died in the forty-eighth year of their marriage.

42

Seven years later, when he was seventy-eight, Philander married Catherine (Jemima) Gallehugh, who was twenty-four. Catherine bore her husband two children, Joe and Annie, the first of whom was born when Philander was eighty.

The young wife Catherine died before the children were ten years old, but Philander outlived her by another eight years. When he was ninety-four, he executed his last will. Written without legal flourishes, it was one of the shortest wills in the history of Madison County, yet it involved extensive properties. Philander bequeathed all of his land and other belongings to Joe and Annie, his teen-aged children.

Philander Goodall died in 1890 at the age of ninety-six. He was buried in the family cemetery on the Goodall Farm.

The valley of Graves Mill flourished, and in 1829 the United States government established a post office, known as Graves, Virginia, at the juncture of the Rapid Ann and Jones Run. Mail was delivered then and for the next eighty years by pack horse. In 1841, after a brief closing, the post office was reopened as Graves Mill, Virginia.

In the meantime, a new settler, Pillar by name, established an apple orchard on rented land at the present-day site of a slab pile near the mouth of McDaniel Hollow. The Pillar orchard—sometimes called Puller and Pillow—lasted for more than a hundred years. (During the period from about 1825 to 1830, the Staunton River was occasionally called Pillar's Prong.)

McDaniel Hollow was known in the early years—and is still known locally—as North New Ground Hollow, named for a new field that the early settlers cleared near the mouth of the hollow on the north slope of Jones Mountain. The upper part of the main hollow branched into three watersheds. The broad, fan-shaped central section became known as Johnsons Ground, apparently named for a mountaineer who occupied a flat near the headsprings. Johnsons Ground extended up the slopes to the top of Church Mountain, touching what is today the Jones Mountain Trail.

Another local landmark was established in 1839, when John Hundley leased a house and sixty acres of land below the hemlocks at the present-day site of another slab pile, where the Staunton River Trail crosses the stream. The crossing was known for the next hundred years as Hundley's Ford.

In the decades before the outbreak of the Civil War, much of Jones Mountain was purchased by valley resident Robert A. Banks, whose ancestors had settled downstream on the Rapid Ann a hundred years earlier. A leading citizen of the area, Banks later served as a general in the Confederate army. He eventually sold his holdings to new arrivals in the area.

Zachariah McDaniel

Settlers meanwhile had moved up the rugged valley of the Conway River—known throughout the area as the Middle River—starting homes in the wide, timbered valley south of Cat Knob and Laurel Gap. Early land patents in the area were acquired in the 1730s by Francis Conway and the Picket family. Part of the area was included in the Big Survey of Thomas Smith. In 1788, the heirs of William Picket sold land at the head of the Conway River to John Brannon.

Most of the homesteads were staked out on the north side of the stream on the lower slopes of Jones Mountain, although members of the Bush family occupied the steep, rugged slopes of the main Blue Ridge Divide. A switchback trail was constructed from the Conway up to Laurel Gap and down into the valley of the Laurel Prong below Cat Knob.

It was to this wild and rugged country that Irishman Zachariah McDaniel came in the early 1800s, migrating east from the Shenandoah Valley. As a young man, Zachariah often climbed the steep pitch to the forested area at Laurel Gap, where he met an Indian girl named Osby. Her family, apparently descendants of the Manahoecs, lived below the gap on the Laurel Prong. A courtship blossomed between Zachariah and Osby, and they were married about 1815. Later, they moved to a house below Cat Knob, known in the early years as Big Cat Knob, in the upper Conway valley. There, in his later years, Zachariah presided as patriarch of the McDaniel family.

Zachariah's son Stacy lived in a log house on cleared land near the mouth of Bootens Run. Stacy's first wife died young. Later, he married Adalein Breeden, who was born in the Conway valley about 1818. Adalein left her mark on the area, bearing eighteen children and living to the age of 105. Today, a cemetery is located on a flat above the former site of Stacy and Adalein McDaniel's home.

In the early years, a corn mill was located on the upper Conway River at the end of a spur road below Lighted Top Mountain. Across the way on Jones Mountain, a maple-syrup sugaring plantation was located in Sugar Hollow, high on the south slope of the mountain at an elevation above 3,000 feet. The upper part of the plantation came almost to the Jones Mountain Trail. A wagon road passed through the hollow connecting with Bootens Run and Bluff Mountain. The same road connected with the Jones Mountain Trail on the north, then continued as a horse trail around the contours of Little Cat Knob, finally ending at the Sag. From the Sag, a wagon road (the present-day Fork Mountain Trail) descended to the Laurel Prong, connecting there with the Laurel Gap trail and a road up the Blue Ridge Divide to Milam Gap.

The old haunts of Zachariah McDaniel and Osby are today in Shenandoah National Park. The sites of the mill, the sugar maple plantation, the cemetery, and the home place of Stacy and Adalein McDaniel are in the Rapidan Wildlife Management Area. Part of the old sugar maple plantation is located at the edge of the park. Most of the roads and trails are now abandoned, and some sections have disappeared.

Old home site of Stacy and Adalein McDaniel, now known as the Booten place, near the mouth of Bootens Run on the Conway River. The house was destroyed by fire in the 1940s. The McDaniels are buried on a hill behind the cabin site.

James Earl McDaniel, sixth generation descendant of Zachariah and Osby McDaniel. As a boy, Jim met his great great grandmother Adalein McDaniel, Zachariah's daughter-in-law, who lived to be 105.

The Mid-1800s: William Jenkins

Chief among the new settlers in the Staunton River Valley was William Jenkins, who in April of 1852 purchased ninety-five acres of land that included part of Bush Field. Jenkins, his wife Juria (whom he married in 1838), and their children, lived in a two-story log cabin across the valley on the north side of the Staunton about one and a half miles from the Rapid Ann River. The cabin was on cleared land near a spring on the slopes of Fork Mountain about 700 feet above the river, reached by a wagon road that crossed a ford on the Staunton River. From the door of his cabin, Jenkins could look directly up to the monolithic Rock Church.

It was to William and Juria's credit that they survived the first harsh winters. Deep snow fell in 1854. Then, beginning on January 19, 1857, the worst storm of the nineteenth century ravaged across Jones Mountain. In the valley, Jenkins and other farmers huddled with their families in their small log cabins. As the storm unleashed its fury, snow drifted to fifteen feet on the cleared slopes below the mountain. Cattle gathered in barns or sheds or wherever they could find shelter.

William Jenkins and his neighbors learned to cope with the elements and the hard life of subsistence farming. In those years, less than half a dozen families lived in the Jones Mountain country. The Estes family owned the former home place of Willis and Clarissa Bush on the south bank of the Staunton. In 1848, ten members of the Nicholson family moved to a mountain tract adjoining Jenkins' land high above Bush Field. Downstream, Milton Eddins lived on his family's domain. The McDaniels lived up the valley. Farther upstream, the Staunton River Valley was still wild and forested.

The mountain people lived in chestnut log cabins, some with massive fireplaces and rock chimneys. A barn, a springhouse, a cellar, a few sheds, and some animal pens were nearby. The sloping fields of the Staunton valley were divided by split-rail fences. For the most part, the farmers lived off the land, but they sold a few crops and other produce commercially. They cultivated gardens and truck patches and grew tobacco, oats, rye, barley, buckwheat, apples, and corn. They also raised chickens, turkeys, and geese. Cattle and sheep grazed the gentle slopes near the river. Hogs roamed free over the mountains. The farmers kept enough horses for plowing and pulling wagons.

The principal economic asset of the mountains was the American chestnut tree, which in those years composed about sixty percent of the Jones Mountain forest. The farmers gathered the chestnuts in the fall and sold them to a produce store in Graves Mill, getting enough income to purchase clothing and shoes for the approaching winter. The nuts yielded good profits early in the season, but later the prices sometimes dropped as much as ninety percent.

The chestnut trees had other uses. "They built their houses with the chestnut logs and covered the roofs with chestnut shingles. They'd last a long time. And chestnut was the only means they had of building their fences," said Buck Hawkins, grandson of William Jenkins.

The farmers also fed chestnuts to hogs, which were butchered and sold for additional income. "It didn't cost a cent to raise chestnuts or hogs in those days," said Johnnie Shifflett, a descendant of the McDaniels. "It was a very inexpensive way to farm. The people made money and had meat on the table too."

Fresh ham was salted down in boxes during cold weather—usually about the first of December—and left for about six weeks. Then the ham was hung in a meat house, where a low fire of hickory wood smoked the meat for several hours. The hickory gave the ham, and sometimes the man who tended the fire, a real smoke flavor.

The Civil War

When the storm clouds of civil war came in 1861, the able-bodied men of Jones Mountain went off to join the regiments of the Army of Northern Virginia. Major battles raged within forty miles of Graves Mill. Troops crossed the Blue Ridge just north of Big Meadows, and General Stonewall Jackson camped on the river bottoms four miles from Jones Mountain. The high summit of Fork Mountain was used as a signaling station by both the Confederate and Federal armies. Deserters from both sides sought refuge in the back hollows, and at least one Federal soldier was hunted down and shot in the hollow of the Haunted Branch. One resident of the Conway Valley who objected to fighting spent four years holed up in a cave near a spring on the east side of Bluff Mountain. On the ridge crest, a few hundred feet above the cave, he built a 30-foot observation tower, stabilized by three guy wires.

Hard times came to northern Virginia after the Civil War. Social, economic, and political institutions collapsed. Banks were closed, currency was devalued, slave labor was brought to an end, and the white labor force was demoralized. Many of the local people—not to mention the slaves themselves—were glad to see slavery end. In 1832, the voters of Madison County had split evenly on a referendum to free the slaves, and a motion in the Virginia general assembly lost by just one vote. In 1840, slaves in Madison County composed 55 percent of the population, but by 1850 the number of slaves was down by about one third. Staunton River landowner Milton Eddins owned several slaves, including "a Negro Girl

Slave for life, named Elizabeth," according to the records, whom he had purchased in 1845 at a price of $314.85. The planters were brought down by the Federal victory, but the effects of Reconstruction were relatively mild among the self-sufficient farmers of Jones Mountain.

John L. Jenkins

Among the men who enlisted in the Confederate army was nineteen-year-old John L. Jenkins, son of William and Juria Jenkins. After the war, John Jenkins returned home to become the proprietor of the family compound on the Staunton River. His father William died in 1866. During the next ten years, John Jenkins lived in the old Willis Bush (later James Estes) place above the high bank on the south side of the river. After the death of his mother Juria in 1877, John sold the Willis Bush parcel to William Utz and moved across the river to the Jenkins home place. There he lived until 1894.

John Jenkins' first wife, Sarah Elizabeth, died during childbirth. Then in 1878, when he was thirty-five, John married Comora Nichols, who was twenty-one. She was the daughter of Albert Nichols of Graves Mill and a sister of twelve-year-old Harvey Nichols.

The Jenkins home on the Staunton River was alive with activity in the 1880s and '90s, when John and Comora began rearing a family of nine children, including a son (Aubrey) from John's first marriage. The other children were Acey, Edith, Gaston, Neddie, Trent, Carey, Wilmer, and Sally. Jenkins farmed a truck patch and raised tobacco, corn, oats, and cabbage. He sold cured tobacco at 10¢ a pound. Jenkins also grew pippin apples in orchards near the cabin and across the river on the upper edge of Bush Field, just below a split-rail fence on the switchback trail. He frequently fished for brook trout, sometimes using a trap seine, which he stretched across the pools and riffles of the Staunton River.

John Jenkins' livestock grazed bluegrass in the summer and ate corn fodder in the winter. In the fall of the year, they also ate persimmons. "Persimmon was the best cattle feed there ever was—got sugar in them," said Charles Jenkins, grandson of John Jenkins. "Up in the mountains there wasn't much hay, but they fed rye and oats to the stock. They cut the oats by hand with a cradle, shocked it in bundles, and put it in a stack, then beat it with sticks. They didn't have binders or threshing machines in the mountains."

Young Comora Jenkins had little time to relax. She cooked over the fireplace but also used a cast-iron wood burner. She made butter by churning cream in a fruit jar. She made her own soap and washed clothes on a scrub board propped up in a tub. In the years after 1886, she sometimes climbed the switchback trail to the top of the mountain, where she visited her brother Harvey.

In June of 1894, John and Comora moved to the Graves Mill Valley, where they bought a 136-acre farm on the north side of Jones Run. There, John started a new apple orchard and grew wheat, barley, and hemp. He also continued farming his land on the Staunton River, going there regularly by horse and wagon to tend the orchards and look after his cattle and sheep.

Tragedy struck the Jenkins family that first year at Graves Mill. In the fall of the year, just after they had garnered their first harvest, Comora Jenkins contracted typhoid fever. She died on November 1, 1894, at the age of thirty-five. She was buried near an evergreen tree on a small knoll in the foothills of Jones Mountain.

John L. Jenkins, who lived on the Staunton River from 1852 until 1894.

In the 1880s, the name of the Staunton River changed again, this time to Wilson Run, the name by which it is still known locally. The side stream known earlier as Wilson Run was left without a name. Surveyors did not consistently adopt the new usage. Land records of the period referred to the main stream by several names, including Wilson Run, the South Fork, the Staunton, the Rapid Ann, "the south prong of the rapid-Ann," and simply "the run." But the people who lived there called it Wilson Run.

In 1933, the National Board of Geographic Names officially restored the name Staunton River to the main stream. A 1933 U.S. Geological Survey Map also restored the name Wilson Run to the side stream.

Another place name that changed in the 1880s was Church Mountain, the northeast arm of Jones Mountain, which took on the name Bear Church Mountain. The ridge behind the summit was often called Bear Hunting Ridge, a name that surveyors sometimes also applied to the entire crest of Jones Mountain, including the crest leading to Bluff Mountain. The name of the Rock Church then evolved into Bear Church. Hikers today refer to it as Bear Church Rock, the name by which it is now identified on maps. The shorter name Bear Church is still used locally. In 1933, the National Board of Geographic Names officially recognized the names Bear Church Mountain and Bear Church Rock.

In 1895, the National Board of Geographic Names changed the name Rapid Ann to Rapidan. Today, the local pronunciation is still Rapid-Ann.

Calvin and Elic McDaniel

Upstream about a mile from the Jenkins farm on the Staunton River (or Wilson Run) lived Calvin McDaniel, one of the eighteen children of Stacy and Adalein and grandson of Zachariah and Osby. The McDaniel home was in a field on the north side of the river, across from a side road that led down from the Staunton River Valley road. There, in the 1870s and early 80s, Calvin McDaniel and his wife reared five children: Elic, Tom, Ed, Maggie, and Calvin, Jr. Calvin ran cattle and sheep on the open slopes behind the house and grew grain crops, apples, and cherries.

The shadows of tragedy descended twice on the McDaniel family. The hard-working Calvin McDaniel died before his children were grown. Then about 1885, fire swept through the home, destroying the house and all of the family's belongings. The family kept the land but did not rebuild. Elic McDaniel moved to the home territory of the McDaniels on the Conway River. Tom and Maggie ("Miss Mag") moved with their mother to the top of Chapman Mountain on the Wilhite Wagon Road (now an abandoned trail in Shenandoah National Park, paralleling the Hoover Road, which was built later). Their home was near a spring about a thousand feet west of the present-day Blakey Ridge Fire Road. Ed McDaniel moved to the old Tom Graves place near Graves Mill but continued farming the Staunton River fields, holding title there until the establishment of the national park.

In the meantime, a young man from the Conway River staked out some land and built a log cabin in the upper reaches of North New Ground Hollow near the top of Jones Mountain. He was Elic McDaniel, a cousin of the Elic McDaniel on the Staunton River. Elic settled on the mountain with his bride Lydia in the early 1870s. Their cabin, a two-story structure, was nestled near a spring at an elevation of nearly 3,000 feet. It was there that Elic and Lydia began rearing their family, four sons and four daughters, one of whom was Mary, who was later to be the wife of Will Shifflett.

A trail, later improved for two-horse wagons, came up to the cabin from the lower hollow and continued across a flat to Garth Spring, about a thousand feet from the cabin at the headwaters of Back Field Hollow. From the spring, another path extended on across Jones Mountain to the hollow of Bootens Run. A spur trail in North New Ground Hollow climbed to the left through Johnsons Ground to the crest of the mountain, then dropped steeply down the other side to the Nichols cabin. Another trail, lying midway between the Garth Spring and Nichols routes, ascended to the ridge, then dropped into Kinsey Hollow. All of the trails are now grown over, and some exist only as traces.

Elic did not clear the land or till the soil. He worked on a farm near the Rapidan River, walking each day down North New Ground Hollow, then out the Staunton Valley road, a round trip of about eight miles. Lydia and Elic remained only a few years at the mountain cabin. The winters were harsh on the northeast slope, and snow was slow to melt. The cycle of winter thaws turned the ground into a quagmire when the soil was not frozen.

The couple eventually returned to the Conway River. There, Lydia died while she was still relatively young. In later decades, the grandchildren of Elic and Lydia McDaniel referred to the old log cabin site as Granddaddy Hollow. To the outside world it became known as McDaniel Hollow.

"Miss Mag" McDaniel (left), her brother Tom, and niece Ollie McDaniel in 1949. Miss Mag and Tom grew up on the Staunton River and moved to Chapman Mountain when their house burned.

Elic McDaniel, the man after whom McDaniel Hollow is named. He and his bride Lydia settled near the top of Jones Mountain in the early 1870s. Photo was made several years later.

Old foundation of log cabin near the top of Jones Mountain, where Elic and Lydia McDaniel lived in the 1870s and '80s.

The present-day McDaniel Hollow Trail should not be confused with the old trails of McDaniel (formerly North New Ground) Hollow. The McDaniel Hollow Trail begins in McDaniel Hollow, just across the stream from the old North New Ground Hollow Trail, but ascends in another direction, passing eventually through Walnut Hollow, which was part of the Calvin McDaniel tract. Calvin used the trail for access by wagon to a field in Walnut Hollow.

Community Life on Jones Mountain

The mountaineers and farmers could always find an excuse for fun and festivity. They gathered for weddings, house raisings, and sometimes civic festivals. One of the biggest celebrations in the area's history was held at Graves Mill in the Centennial Year of 1876. People arrived from all around, riding horseback or traveling in wagons and buggies. Picnic lunches were spread on makeshift tables. Chairs were brought in for the elderly. Quilts were spread for the young. It was a day of bustling activity by people who for the most part had known one another all their lives. Laughter and good humor filled the air. Noisy children ran about. Tournaments were held and winners were announced. Young Linda Graves was crowned the Queen of Love and Beauty. And the highlight of the event came as people gathered to hear a speech by former Confederate General Robert A. Banks, one of their own hometown boys.

Quilting parties were a favorite pastime of the mountain women. They gathered at homes, sitting around a quilting board to stitch the fabrics into elaborate patchwork. They usually brought their children. The events were grand social occasions, with ample opportunity for talking. Some of the older women, being of a more dignified mind, merely sat quietly and smoked pipes.

Hunting was the major sport for men and boys. They often hunted bears on the tableland and the outlying ridges, including Bluff Mountain, the Jones Mountain point above Graves Mill, and Bear Hunting Ridge. But the best bear hunting was in the undeveloped timberland of the upper Staunton River Valley, the place that everyone called the Wilderness.

"The people used to go up there in the Wilderness and hunt bear," Charles Jenkins said. "They built some bear stands in the hemlocks about four feet off the ground and led old horses up on the stands. Then they shot the horses as bait and hid in the brush, and then they shot the bears that came to feed on the horses."

(Uncontrolled hunting eventually killed off the bear population. By the early 1900s, they were gone. "We never saw a bear in all the years we lived there," said Johnnie Shifflett, grandson of Elic McDaniel. Overhunting in the nineteenth century also wiped out the deer and elk populations of Jones Mountain and the valleys. A hundred years earlier, the settlers had eliminated the mountain lions and wolves.)

The people often attended church services on the Sabbath Day and prayer meetings during the week. For a few years, a Methodist church was located on the east side of the Rapidan River, a mile north of Graves Mill, across from where State Route 662 makes its final turn toward Jones Mountain. The Baptists, who had established the Rapid Ann Meetinghouse in 1773, continued as the principal denomination in the

Detail of a patch work bed cover made at a quilting party near Jones Mountain in the early 1900s.

Graves Mill Valley. On October 14, 1886, the Shiloh Baptist Association opened the Graves Chapel at Graves Mill with thirty charter members. Organ music, singing, and preaching drew such large crowds that the congregation often overflowed into the church yard.

Revivals were held in the fall of the year. "We always had visiting preachers, and we'd walk down there at night with our lanterns. All the people back in the mountains went to church, and we'd have right smart crowds," said Effie McDaniel, who attended the church in the early 1900s.

A two-room school was also at Graves Mill, offering education through the eighth grade. Boys and girls were taught in separate rooms and had separate play periods. Effie McDaniel walked to the school from her family's home on the Staunton River. "I had to leave early in the morning when it was still dark," she said. "My mother walked me down to the Big Bridge, where I met other children, and then we'd walk on from there. Then my mother met me at the Big Bridge each evening, when it was almost dark."

There were no public high schools in the area, but private schools were available to families who could afford them. In 1880, John D. Fray opened the Warwick School for boys in the Hebron Valley. In 1890, the Rock Springs Institute, a private school for girls, was opened at Shelby. Both schools were about eight miles by road from Graves Mill.

Many of the Jones Mountain children did not attend school. Buck Hawkins, the man of the poem "And by God's Grace," (see p. 88) said he attended school two months a year for two years.

In the 1890s and early 1900s, young people gathered often in the mountain homes for parties and dances and sometimes rode to a dance hall in Wolftown, which was open on Saturday nights. Bob Smith often played lead fiddle at square dances. Bill Via played tenor banjo.

Bob Smith's first performance was at a barn dance in Wolftown in 1897, when he was seventeen. "Those mountain people around Graves Mill liked square dances," Smith said. "They didn't know what a waltz was, but when they'd take two or three drinks of that good spring water, they knew how to dance. They liked something quick. And when I started sawing my fiddle, those mountain fellows got to jumping as high as a table."

In later years, Bob Smith won awards at music festivals and eventually played with the Alexandria String Band, which traveled to dances throughout the area. Smith kept his ties around Graves Mill, where he grazed white-face Herefords on the Jenkins and Goodall farms and bought apple brandy from Harvey Nichols. He was invited several times

56

to play the fiddle at square dances in private homes around Jones Mountain. The dancers usually filled two rooms while Bob Smith sawed off "Old Joe Clark," "Ragtime Annie," "Wabash Cannonball," "Flop-Eared Mule," and other hoe-downs.

Buck Hawkins usually called the figures. Sometimes, while the fiddlers were resting, he stood on a chair and led the group in singing. He

Bob Smith, who played lead fiddle at Wolftown barn dances in 1897 and later at dances in private homes near Graves Mill. Photo was made in 1979 on his 100th birthday.

especially liked "Little Brown Jug," "Hail, Hail, the Gang's All Here," and "Pull Your Shades Down, Mary Ann (if you want to keep your secrets from your future man)."

"Buck Hawkins was a good caller and good dancer and a good man with it," Bob Smith said. Buck was also a good storyteller, and one of his stories was about the dances at Wolftown around 1910. Liquor was

Buck Hawkins, who drove the produce wagon from Graves Mill during the early 1900s. Photo was made about 1961.

always in demand, and the mountain boys usually had it. "When you'd go to Wolftown to a dance, you'd always lose your liquor," Buck said. "Well, I had an old horse that I rode by the name of Charley, and he was an awful vicious looking horse . . . . And I could just slip a quart bottle down between his back and the saddle, and I tied old Charley to a rail and went on about my business. And whenever anybody started for that bottle, the horse laid his ears right back and opened that mouth and rung that tail and got those hind feet a goin', and they never went to that horse."

Some of the good times were spent off the dance floor, and one of the popular activities was lassoing wild hogs. The big animals (descendants of loose domestic stock) could be dangerous, as Elmer Taylor found out when he was attacked by a 300-pound sow protecting a litter of pigs. Elmer scrambled up the nearest tree and stayed there, to his embarrassment, until his hunting companions came to the rescue.

Harvey Nichols, who lived in the Jones Mountain Cabin, usually didn't have to go far to find wild hogs. A favorite shelter for many of the hogs was under an overhanging rock above Harvey's cabin. "We called that place Wild Hog Rock," said Elton Berry. The rock was located in a thicket of laurel just off the trail above the cabin. The top of the rock was just above ground level, forming a bluff overlooking the Staunton Valley.

Elton Berry, who hunted wild hogs on Jones Mountain in the early 1930s. (1981 photo)

"There was a narrow cave-thing under that rock, and wild hogs used to hole up in there," Berry said. "One time, there was a litter of pigs under there, and the sow was gone, and I tied a shoestring onto the end of a long stick and reached back in there and snared one of the pigs by the hind leg and pulled that little devil out. Kenny McDaniel put the pig in a flour sack, and we headed down the trail toward Harvey's place. And then that pig started squealing, and that big sow came out of the bushes and charged right at us. Boy, you talk about movin'! We ran as fast as we could, but that sow started gaining on us, and Kenny grabbed hold of a hanging vine just in time and went flying out over the ground, and that sow just barreled right on under him.

"Then we took a rope and got that sow tied up and pulled her down to the Wilson Run [Staunton River] and loaded her onto a wagon with the pig and took both of them to Graves Mill and sold them."

The Lillard Distillery and the Breedens

In 1893, Confederate veteran Howard Lillard moved across the Blue Ridge Mountains from Page County and opened a bonded distillery at the base of Jones Mountain in the Staunton River Valley. He lived on 600 acres of land in the Graves Mill Valley. The Lillard Distillery was not the first bonded distillery in the valley, however. For several years about the time of the Civil War, a distillery was located about a mile up the Staunton River on the north side of the stream, a site marked today by a stone pier at the edge of the river across from the Staunton River trail. There were also two distilleries within two miles of the Staunton—the Kinsey Distillery in Big Kinsey Hollow (operated by John Hawkins and his son Buck) and the Kite Distillery, located just east of the present-day Hoover Bridge on the Rapidan.

The Lillard Distillery, which produced apple brandy, was located on the Willis Bush place, which Howard Lillard purchased from Silas and Fannie Utz, who had lived there for several years. The processing plant was in a large log building on the bank of the river where the creek from the Nichols spring fed into the stream. An orchard of 700 apple trees was behind the home site about a quarter of a mile below the plant.

Dave "Fat" Breeden managed the orchard and the distillery for twenty-four years, from 1893 until 1917. He ground the apples in a horse-powered rotary mill, then fermented the fruit in hogsheads at the distillery. The apple brandy was shipped by wagon to Somerset in fifty-gallon barrels. In addition to the orchard and distillery operations, Dave had to tend his own crops and a vegetable garden. He had two cows and a horse and raised turkeys, chickens, and hogs.

Dave Breeden and his wife Lucy lived above the rock retaining wall on the Staunton River Road in the home previously occupied by the Utz family and before that by John Jenkins. The house was a two-story log structure, twelve by twenty-four feet, with weather-board siding. There were two rooms on each floor. A basement where vegetables were stored was lined with rocks and had a fireplace. A barn, a milk shed, a chicken house, and a corn house were nearby. A small springhouse was off to the side.

The Breedens had two daughters, Mamie and Effie, born in 1894 and 1904. The daughters did their share of the work. "I used to sit in the basement by a kerosene lamp peeling apples till ten o'clock at night," Effie recalled. She milked the cows every morning before sunrise and at night after returning from school. Effie and Mamie also worked in the fields. "I planted corn in the new grounds. I'd get so tired, I'd lay down on the rocks," Effie said.

The Breedens did not spend all their time working. Every week or so, they hitched up the family buggy and rode to Graves Mill or Madison. They also attended fish fries and soups, which were usually held on the river banks where the Staunton met the Rapidan. These gatherings always drew lots of people, some of whom hiked on up to Bear Church to take in the view. In the evenings, the Breeden girls sometimes dated boyfriends. "Any time you went out with a boy, your mother and father would be right behind you with a lantern," Effie said.

In 1912, at the age of eighteen, Mamie married twenty-one year old Charles "Charley" Knighting, whose family lived on the south side of Doubletop Mountain about a half mile up a side road from the Rapidan River, just above the second (present-day) bridge. Knighting delivered mail on horseback to the Graves Mill and Rockland post offices. Charley and Mamie lived near the Staunton River, just across the stream from the present-day PATC cabin parking lot. The house had been previously occupied by Stonewall Graves and earlier by John Graves. A wooden footbridge crossed the Staunton near the house. At this home, Mamie bore her husband three daughters, the eldest of whom was Marie.

The children would not have a mother for long. In 1920, Mamie Knighting contracted pneumonia and died within a few days. She was twenty-six. They buried her in a small cemetery above the Big Bridge on the lower slope of Jones Mountain.

In 1919, Effie Breeden married Claude McDaniel, son of Ed McDaniel, who farmed the Staunton River fields. They were both sixteen. The young couple lived at a logging camp just behind the present-day PATC parking lot. Later, they moved to the Lillard place, then back downstream to the Knighting (or Graves) house, where they lived until

61

the national park acquired the land. Dave and Lucy Breeden also lived for a while in the Knighting house, then moved beyond Graves Mill. Dave Breeden survived to the age of ninety-seven.

Howard Lillard with grandson Hume in 1914. From 1893 to 1918, Lillard operated a bonded distillery on the Staunton River below the Nichols side stream.

Rock pier on the Staunton River, all that is left of another bonded distillery that operated about the time of the Civil War.

Charles Knighting, twenty-one, and Mamie Breeden, eighteen, on their wedding day in 1912. They lived on the Staunton River near the confluence with the Rapidan.

Claude and Effie (Breeden) McDaniel. They lived on the Staunton River.

The Produce Riders

A general store with a hitching rail out front was located at Graves Mill (later, there were two other stores) where about every imaginable item could be purchased. The inventory included fruit jars, flatirons, hats, shoes, saddles, lanterns, watches, cod-liver oil, and roll-your-own tobacco. Also available were food staples, kitchenware, clothing, and various patent medicines. The store was also the social center of Graves Mill and the Jones Mountain area. People congregated regularly in a circle of chairs around a potbellied stove.

The farmers brought their produce to the store, where it was shipped by wagon to Somerset (earlier to Gordonsville) and by rail to Baltimore. In the fall of the year, two wagon loads of chestnuts were hauled from Graves Mill every week. The wagons operated full time throughout the year, carrying out produce and bringing in merchandise for the store. Usually, the same containers were used for the return trip. A barrel packed with dressed chickens for shipment to Baltimore might come back filled with sugar. Some of the produce was shipped longer distances. Apples were picked green from the Staunton River orchards and taken by wagon and rail to Baltimore and then by ship across the Atlantic to Liverpool, England.

The wagon trip to Somerset took two days for the thirty-six mile round trip. Four horses were used to pull the big wagons loaded with heavy cargo. Two men hitched up the horses, loaded the produce, and pulled out of Graves Mill before daybreak. The teamsters carried their food and personal gear in a wooden box attached to the wagon. They drove hard on the rough roads all day, stopping only to feed, water, and rest the horses. They crossed eighteen stream fords on a route that took them through Wolftown, Shelby, Shifflett's Corner, and Rochelle. At Shifflett's Corner and Rochelle, other produce wagons fed onto the road, some pulled by oxen, all bound for Somerset. Melvin Aylor, who lived on the Blue Ridge Turnpike at Madison, once counted twenty-seven wagons in one day.

The Graves Mill teamsters usually reached Somerset at five o'clock in the afternoon. They unloaded the produce at a warehouse alongside the railroad, then fed hay and corn to the horses. The men made camp for the night on a flat just above the rail siding. On an average night, about fifty teamsters camped at the site. "We built campfires and warmed our grub, usually meat and beans and pie, and stood around the fires almost all night," said Dewey Shifflett, who hauled apples, sheep, and hogs direct from his farm on the Staunton River.

One winter night about 1912, teamster Buck Hawkins took coal

65

Graves Mill photo made in 1979 shows old Utz General Store and post office. Buildings further down the road include an earlier store and post office, a blacksmith shop, a school building, and the Graves Chapel. Another general store (near the present-day post office) was destroyed by fire. All buildings except Graves Chapel are now abandoned. Bluff Mountain, an arm of Jones Mountain, is in background.

Four-horse produce wagons pausing near Rochelle en route to an overnight camp at Somerset in the early 1900s.

from the warehouse and added it to the fire to make it hotter. "We'd slip Old Man Bill Butler's coal, and he'd come out there in the night raisin' hell about burnin' his coal and give us a lecture about that, and we'd just listen." Bill Butler was the produce buyer at Somerset.

The teamsters usually slept in their wagons, which were protected from the elements by canvas covers. A few men pitched tents. Some nights, trains came blasting through Somerset, waking the teamsters and terrifying the horses, some of which were not stabled. "One night, a train came through there just a flyin', and the horses took off . . . . We found them about a mile and a half away," said Joe Fray, who hauled produce from Hebron.

On the morning of the second day, the Graves Mill crew usually broke camp before dawn, loaded the wagon with supplies for the store, and rumbled off toward home. "We usually had a smaller load coming back. The horses were anxious to get back home, and they moved a little bit faster going back," produce rider Buck Hawkins said.

The Frays

By this time, seven generations had passed since 1748, when George Hume surveyed Garth Spring and the bluegrass field on the top of Jones Mountain. Throughout the period, the parcel was known as the Garth Spring tract, even though its boundaries extended far beyond the spring and the field. The tract also took in most of the western mountain crest and the vast untouched forest of hemlocks, oaks, and chestnuts in the upper Staunton Valley—the area known as the Wilderness. When John D. Fray, his brother Hamp, and two partners purchased the 1,122-acre parcel on the first day of January in 1891, the land was still undeveloped except for a horse trail up the valley to the Sag, a partly constructed trail along the slope of Little Cat Knob, and a stock path known today as the Jones Mountain Trail.

The Frays and their partners owned a total of 3,089 acres of Blue Ridge Mountain land. Besides the Wilderness (or Garth Spring) tract, they owned 900 acres of grazing land adjacent to the Spitler tract on Haywood (sometimes called Hayward) Mountain—known today as Spitler Hill—and more than a thousand acres in Dark Hollow, where fourteen squatter families resided. (The three tracts are today part of the national park.)

The original Fray family settled in the German community of Hebron in 1792. From 1880 to 1915, John Fray ran the Warwick School and raised short-horn cattle on a large farm in the Hebron Valley. During the summer months, he grazed the cattle on the Garth Spring tract and

Spitler Hill. For several years, Rubin McDaniel, a grandson of Zachariah, tended the cattle on Jones Mountain. Rubin trained the stock to come in off the trails when he blew a fox horn.

One of Fray's students was his son Joe, who later graduated from Roanoke College and became the treasurer of Madison County. Joe Fray eventually took over the cattle operations and spent all of his spare time in the mountains. Each spring, he drove about fifty head of cattle to the Garth Spring Field, herding the cows through Graves Mill, then up the Staunton River Road, and on up a narrow trail in Back Field Hollow (along Garth Spring Run) to the bluegrass field. On the cattle drives, Joe used dogs to keep the stock in line. "Dogs are better than people for driving cattle," he said.

During the Frays' proprietorship of the Wilderness, only one acre of the forest was cut. In the 1890s, Adam Hurt cleared a small field near the Sag and started to haul out timber until he found out that he did not own the land. The tiny clearing, known in later years as the Adam Hurt Field, was about 500 feet south of where the present-day trails come together at the Sag.

The Frays kept the Wilderness about forty-five years, then sold the land to the new Shenandoah National Park. The thousand-acre tract had survived as a primeval forest during 200 years of private ownership.

Jones Mountain landowner John D. Fray sits for photo with his students at Warwich School in 1907. Fray owned the hemlock Wilderness tract and Garth Spring Field. Son Joe Fray is on front row, far right.

Joe Fray in 1915, as a student at Roanoke College. Later, he owned 3,000 acres of land in what is now the Shenandoah National Park, including Dark Hollow, part of Spitler Hill, and the Staunton River Wilderness.

The Shifflett Family

In the years when John and Joe Fray drove cattle up the valley to
Garth Spring, they sometimes stopped briefly at a small white cottage
beside the road, nearly three miles up the Staunton River Valley. There,
on the old Pillar place, lived Will T. Shifflett, who in his time would
become the leading farmer and landowner in the middle Staunton Valley.
Will Shifflett was born in 1868 and grew up on the Lancaster place on
Garth Run. About 1888, he married young Lisa Breeden, a daughter of
Tom Breeden. The newlyweds moved to the upper Conway River, where
they settled in a log cabin just across the stream from the old Conway
Road.

Will and Lisa's life together began with happiness and great expecta-
tions but ended in tragedy just thirteen months later. Lisa was expecting a
child, and as the day approached, women in the area made preparations
to assist in the delivery. The sky had been sunny, but storm clouds
gathered unexpectedly, and a torrent of rain turned the Conway into a
rampaging flood just as Lisa Shifflett felt the first pains of childbirth.
Will Shifflett called for help, and the women tried desperately to get

**The Garth Spring Field on the top of Jones Mountain, 1926. Land is now
in Shenandoah National Park, where the Jones Mountain Trail crosses
the tableland.**

across the swollen river. But there was no way they could make it, and Lisa died as the women stood helplessly on the opposite bank.

A few years later, Will Shifflett married Mary McDaniel, one of the daughters of Elic, after whom McDaniel Hollow was named. Their first home was on the Collins place on Garth Run. During the 1890s, the couple lived for a while in the Lillard house, just before Dave Breeden occupied the place. Then Will purchased the 264-acre Pillar tract and moved to the little white house, a log structure with weather boarding on the outside and a chimney at one end. The house was near the mouth of McDaniel Hollow. Across the road was the old Pillar orchard of red delicious apples (today the site of a lumber slab pile).

The Shiffletts had eleven children: Mamie, Melvin, Maude, Dewey, Bernice (a boy), Elsie, Homer, Clyde, Laura, Nina, and Johnnie. About 1915, the family moved to the old William Jenkins log cabin, a mile down the river. Will and his older boys built a two-story frame addition on the east side of the cabin. Charles Gray constructed a new chimney on the addition, about the same size as the old chimney on the west end. Later, Will and son Homer constructed a rock retaining wall behind the house, then built a one-story addition to the back of the house for a kitchen, a dining area, and a pantry. A porch was added to the front of the new house. When the new house was finished, they painted it white.

All of the sloping land around the house was cleared. Meadows and corn fields extended from the Staunton River to nearly the top of Fork Mountain, and part of the high ridge line was cleared. Will and Mary cultivated a large garden on the west side of the house. Several pear trees grew near the old chimney. A peach orchard was behind the house. "Anything you could raise to eat, we had it," son Dewey said. His brother Johnnie said that raising vegetables was simpler then. "The bugs didn't both the bean patches in those years," he said. "Nowadays, you have to spray with insecticides."

Thirty feet east of the dwelling stood a springhouse, where Will Shifflett kept two sixteen-gallon milk cans in a pool of cold water. Also near the dwelling were a barn, a smokehouse, and a corn house. A footpath from the compound extended up to the top of Fork Mountain and down to the Rapidan River, and several of the Shifflett children walked to school on the path.

When Will and Mary had moved in 1915, Will kept the cottage and apple orchard in McDaniel Hollow. Later, he bought the Will Gallehugh house, about a half mile downstream from the Jenkins place, just behind the old distillery pier. This acquisition brought Will Shifflett's land holdings to nearly 400 acres, which included about two miles of fields along the Staunton River. He grew rye grass in the fields and grazed thirty sheep and a few horses and milk cows. He also had eighty hogs and a hundred chickens. He owned an apple orchard with 236 trees in the old Bush Field.

Will Shifflett shipped out produce from August until well into the winter, beginning with apples and peaches, then chestnuts, and later hogs and sheep. In the late fall of the year, Will's sons butchered about ten hogs, salted the meat down, and got it ready for shipping. The sheep were shipped live. Son Dewey drove the family's produce wagon to Somerset. He left the Staunton River farm at three in the morning and passed through Graves Mill about the same time that the produce riders from the store were pulling out. "We made good money at it," Dewey said. "More than any of us has ever made since."

For relaxation, Will Shifflett hunted squirrels and coons with a double-barreled shotgun. He and his sons also fished for trout in the Staunton River (which everyone called Wilson Run). "That was the best stream in the county," son Johnnie said. "I caught thirty-five or forty fish in just one day. It wouldn't take any time at all to catch a trout." Johnnie's favorite fishing hole was a deep pool beside the ford where the Shifflett side road crossed the stream. He often fished from a big rock just above the pool.

Another good pastime was visiting neighbors, the closest of whom in those years were Fat Breeden, Claude McDaniel, Will Gallehugh, and Harvey Nichols. Will and the boys often crossed Bush Field and climbed the switchback trail to Harvey's cabin. But Harvey didn't always bother to come down the mountain when he had something to say. A man with a booming voice, he simply climbed to the flat above his cabin and yelled out his messages. "We could hear him good across the valley," Dewey Shifflett said. "He usually wanted to know if we had seen his dogs."

As Will's children grew up, some of them stayed in the valley to start their own farms. Homer Shifflett married Ruby Breeden in 1929 and moved with his bride into the old Lillard place above the retaining wall on the valley road. "I had a real nice garden right on the corner of that high bank beside the road," Homer said.

Will's daughter Laura married Charley Flinchem. The couple lived for a while in the Shifflett's Gallehugh house behind the old distillery pier, then moved to what was then called the Evans place on the Rapidan, the same place occupied by Joel and Lydia Eddins more than a hundred years earlier. Charley was an accomplished musician who played the organ, fiddle, banjo, guitar, accordion, and autoharp.

Daughter Elsie Shifflett married Sydney Allen, a lumberjack with the West Virginia Timber Company, which was then harvesting timber on Jones Mountain. Sydney and Elsie moved into the Shifflett's white cottage at the mouth of McDaniel Hollow. There they remained for several years, rearing four daughters: Lillian, Catherine, Mary Lea, and Estelle. After the timber harvest, Sydney farmed the land and worked at odd jobs. For a while, he looked after Joe Fray's cattle on the Garth Spring Field.

Sydney Allen disappeared mysteriously in the late 1920s. He left the house one morning on a routine trip by horseback to a store in Criglersville. Later that day, riders on Chapman Mountain saw the horse without a rider. The reins were tied loosely to the saddle horn. The horse was returning to Jones Mountain on the old Criglersville Road (now an abandoned grade in the national park, passing over Chapman Mountain a half mile south of the Hoover Road). Crossing the Rapidan on the Big Bridge, the horse plodded on up the Staunton River Road to the Allen home.

Sydney Allen was not seen that day in Criglersville. Search parties failed to turn up clues, and eventually the case was closed.

In the meantime, Johnnie Shifflett married Marie Knighting, the oldest daughter of Charles and Mamie Knighting. Johnnie and Marie lived in the Shifflett family home helping Will and Mary Shifflett, who were then in their sixties. The family ties were close, and every Sunday all the children and grandchildren gravitated to the home place, where meals were served to sometimes upwards of thirty people.

Dewey Shifflett lived for a while in Orange, then returned with his wife Suzie to the Shifflett home on the Staunton River. In 1939, they were the last people to leave the area. (See page 11.)

Fishing hole on the Staunton River, known locally as Wilson Run. Johnnie Shifflett fished from the same rock where man is sitting.

Courtesy of the Shifflett family.

Lisa Shifflett about 1888,
first wife of Will Shifflett.
She died in childbirth
when neighbors could not
get across a flooding
stream to aid her.

Courtesy of the Shifflett family.

Will Shifflett
about 1890.

Laura Shifflett, about age twenty, standing on the steps of the Shifflett home on the Staunton River. Her parents were Will and Mary (McDaniel) Shifflett.

Three of Sydney and Elsie Allen's children with their grandparents, Will and Mary Shifflett. Standing, Lillian (left) and Estelle Allen. Their younger brother Hollis is sitting on Will Shifflett's lap. The children were born and reared about three miles up the Staunton River, known to them as Wilson Run.

The Criglersville Road, now an abandoned trail in Shenandoah National Park. Here, Sydney Allen's horse was seen returning to Jones Mountain without a rider. The old road later was part of a blue-blazed trail, opened in the 1930s by Charley Thomas of the Potomac Appalachian Trail Club.

Photo shows part of the cottage on the Staunton River where Sydney Allen and his wife Elsie lived. Joe Fray is standing between the Allens.

77

Johnnie Shifflett examines shotgun used by his father Will Shifflett while hunting on Jones Mountain before the establishment of Shenandoah National Park.

Dewey and Suzy Shifflett, the last people to leave the Jones Mountain area when the national park was established. Dewey, a son of Will Shifflett, lived for forty years below Bear Church Rock. Suzy was born and reared in Weakley Hollow. Photo was made five weeks before Dewey's death in May 1980.

Retaining wall and one of two chimneys at the site of the Shifflett home today.

The Chestnut Blight

In the year 1918, the chestnut blight began to spread its silent death across Jones Mountain. Within four years, thousands of dead trees stood as testimony to a time when more than half the forest was American chestnut. October became a time of haunting memories as the mountaineers recalled the big nut harvests of years past.

Oak eventually replaced the chestnut as the dominant tree of the Jones Mountain forest. Chestnut shoots continued to grow from the roots, but saplings seldom attained a height of more than fifteen feet before the blight brought them down.

One of the chestnuts had been the largest tree of the Jones Mountain forest. Some seven to nine feet in diameter, it had become something of a landmark on the edge of the valley road a few hundred feet below Harvey Nichols' wagon road. "That was the biggest damned chestnut that ever grew anywhere," Johnnie Shifflett said. The tree died in the 1920s. The last surviving chestnut on Jones Mountain died in the early 1930s. It stood near Elic McDaniel's old cabin, a thousand feet across the flat from Garth Spring.

The immediate effect of the blight was to deplete the supply of nuts used for livestock feed and wipe out the commercial crop that had been a mainstay of mountain economics. Long-term effects deprived the farmers of a durable wood for posts, rails, and the logs that were used in the construction of buildings. Commercial timber production also suffered, but not until the logging companies had one last fling during the great timber harvests of the 1920s and '30s.

The Timber Harvesters

In 1922, Graves Mill was transformed from a quiet farming village into a bustling loggers' town, when the West Virginia Timber Company built five logging camps in the area and pushed four railroads into the back hollows and along the lower slopes of Jones Mountain. Logging roads were constructed to the rail terminals, and skid roads were cleared to the higher reaches of the mountain. It was an ambitious and costly project but one that would succeed if the loggers could clear-cut enough timber.

The West Virginia Timber Company bought several thousand acres of land, mostly in the Conway and upper Rapidan watersheds, land previously owned by the Eagle Hardwood Lumber Company. The West Virginia company also acquired extensive timber rights in Big Kinsey Hollow and the Staunton River Valley. Other timberlands were acquired near Wolftown.

The narrow-gauge rail line extended from Orange across the Piedmont hills to Wolftown and Graves Mill, with spur lines up Garth Run, Big Kinsey, the Rapidan, and the Staunton. A depot, a rail siding, and a Y-turnaround were located at Wolftown.

A work crew under E.L. Whitlock constructed the roadbeds and installed the rails for the spur lines out of Graves Mill. The ties and tracks were transported on flat-bed cars pulled by a steam-driven locomotive that moved along the new tracks just behind the construction crew. "Our job was to build the track," Whitlock said. "I ran the engine while the men built the roadbed and laid the tracks."

The grades were leveled by scoop pans pulled by horses and mules. On the steeper slopes of Jones Mountain, the workers used dynamite to blast out a roadbed.

Courtesy of Mildred Hoffman.

Narrow-gauge railroad at Wolftown, 1920. The large building was a bank. Spur lines of the railroad extended into the back hollows of Jones Mountain, where logging operations were carried out in the early 1920s

The Staunton River railroad paralleled the valley road for some distance, then switchbacked at Y-turns to the high slopes, and ended at the Wilson Run side stream. One of the logging camps, Brown's Camp, was on the south side of the Staunton River in a field near the present-day trailhead. About twenty lumberjacks and a kitchen crew lived in a long bunkhouse next to a mess hall. Stables for about forty horses were behind the camp. Some loggers, including Dewey Shifflett and Sydney Allen, lived at homes in the valley. A company veterinarian traveled from camp to camp, treating sick and injured horses. "Half of the company horses were no good," Charles Jenkins said. "They were poor stock—runty animals."

The timbering crew was divided into teams. "We had some people cutting, some pulling, some sawing, and some loading," Dewey Shifflett said. "We cut trees up the side of the mountain as far as we could go. I drove a team pulling the logs down." A steam-powered loader at the rail terminal on Wilson Run hoisted the logs onto flat-bed cars. Double-header Dinkeys—two small locomotives—pulled from three to six cars at a time to Wolftown, where fifteen or twenty cars were connected to a large Shay engine for the haul to Orange. "When the Shay engine came through Wolftown, every window rattled," Mildred Whitlock said.

Some of the logs were sawed into lumber at two sawmills in the Staunton Valley and hauled by wagon to the railhead. One sawmill was located on the Staunton River Road where the present-day Jones Mountain Trail begins. A supply shed was located higher on the mountain, just off the Jones Mountain Trail. Another sawmill was located at the Lillard place, operated by a contractor named Chestnut.

Several romances developed among the lumberjacks and the local girls. Harvey Nichols' pretty daughters sometimes trifled with the loggers, but more often they went down to Brown's Camp and slipped horses away for joy rides. One lasting romance got its start at the Chestnut camp, where the widower Charles Knighting worked. Also working there was Vondora Kelly, Chestnut's sister-in-law. Charley was in charge of the horses, and Vondora was in charge of the cows—jobs that brought the couple together in the stables when Vondora milked the cows. After the two got married, they moved to Ohio, where they lived happily for forty-five years.

Most of the logging on Jones Mountain ended in 1925. The West Virginia Timber Company sold its land and some of the timber rights to the Ward-Rue Lumber Company. The railroad was removed about 1928. The total timber harvest on Jones Mountain was extensive, involving clear-cuts in most of the Staunton River Valley, Big Kinsey Hollow, and the Bluff Mountain and Garth Run areas. Parts of the mountain were spared, including Johnsons Ground and most of the ridges. Only a part of the rail line up the Rapidan was used. The engineers would not take the trains onto a bridge across the Staunton River.

In 1936, before the national park took over the land, the Ward-Rue Lumber Company harvested oak, poplar, dead standing chestnuts, and a few hemlocks just below the Wilderness. For several weeks, the company operated a sawmill at Hundleys Ford, a place marked today by the remnants of their slab pile. A logging road was constructed up to the new Fork Mountain Fire Road, where lumber and sawlogs were hauled out.

The slab pile at the mouth of McDaniel Hollow, on Pillar's old orchard land across the road from Sydney Allen's house, resulted from timber operations after the national park was established. In 1939, the Cubbage Company, a contractor for the government, harvested the dead standing chestnuts in the Wilderness, sawed them into lumber at a sawmill in McDaniel Hollow, and hauled the lumber out the valley road. The lumber was used for the construction of cabins and a lodge at Big Meadows.

The Final Years

In the mid-1920s, word began to spread about the establishment of the new Shenandoah National Park, and within a few years, surveyors and land specialists had laid out the boundaries. The Staunton River watershed and most of the adjacent part of the Rapidan Valley were marked for acquisition. The boundary of the new park would run roughly along the crest of Jones Mountain, then circle to take in most of the ridges and hollows around Bear Church. The park would take all of the Wilderness, the McDaniel lands, Sydney Allen's house, the Shifflett farms, the Lillard place, Brown's Camp, the Breeden properties, and half of Chapman and Fork Mountains: altogether, about 5,000 acres in the Jones Mountain area. The entire park would be about a hundred miles long, comprising some 175,000 acres.

The news of the new national park was greeted warmly in Richmond and other Virginia cities. State officials had promoted the idea, and the people of Virginia raised money to purchase the land as a gift to the nation. It was Virginia's first and only big national park, preserving in the Blue Ridge Mountains some of the finest scenery in the eastern United States.

Some Virginians opposed the park, notably those whose lives would be most effected: the mountaineers and farmers who would have to relocate. Their roots were deep. Their way of life was fixed. Many of the people feared for their livelihood in unfamiliar surroundings. "All the people around here were against the park," Effie McDaniel said. Some of the people of the county spoke less kindly: "Those park people were a bunch of scoundrels," Bob Smith said.

Time was running out for the mountain people, but before they could absorb the shock, another event distracted them and brought national publicity to the Rapidan area. In 1929, President Herbert Hoover purchased 160 acres of land on the far side of Fork Mountain and built his summer White House in a hemlock grove where the Laurel Prong and the Mill Prong came together to form the Rapidan River. The old Wilhite Wagon Road was closed, and the new "Hoover" Road was constructed for access to the presidential retreat.

The Rapidan Camp had about ten buildings, including a mess hall, a lounge and recreation hall, guest houses, and a large cabin for the president. Hoover's cabin was a four-room rustic frame structure with exposed two-by-four rafters, ceiling joists, and studs. The cabin did not have a foundation—six-inch wooden piers were merely set on rock slabs. A big L-shaped room had giant fireplaces at each end. All of the president's furniture was pine except wicker chairs that were placed around a large dining table. A long pine sofa and other chairs were covered with cushions. Hoover had a shower but no bathtub.

A separate camp near the Rapidan housed a hundred U.S. Marines, who guarded the area and did construction work. Roads and trails were guarded by army troops, who camped near the Hoover Bridge, a site marked today by a road triangle where the Fork Mountain Fire Road begins.

Work crews built a 35-foot observation tower for the president's guests on the summit of Fork Mountain. For access to the tower, civilian workers constructed what is now the Fork Mountain Fire Road, blasting their way right through the Wilderness. "They used cases and cases of dynamite," Johnnie Shifflett said. "I used to go up when the men ate lunch. The bosses, Watson and Brown, always gave me the empty dynamite boxes—good boxes. I used them to feed cattle out of."

The workers rebuilt the old wagon road (the present-day Fork Mountain Trail) from the Laurel Prong up to the new road at the Sag. Another trail was cleared from Laurel Gap up to the summit of Hazeltop.

During the spring and summer months from 1929 until 1932, President Hoover was usually at the Rapidan Camp from Friday night until Monday morning. Sometimes he brought more than a hundred guests. The motorcade came through Criglersville and across Chapman Mountain on the new Hoover Road, then up the Rapidan to the camp. Guests hiked the trails and rode horseback, frequently climbing to the observation tower. Hoover himself hiked in street shoes, wearing a suit and tie.

The presidential mail was delivered by airplane to a landing field near Syria. Urgent mail was sometimes dropped to the ground near the Rapidan until one day, according to Joe Fray, when the mail bag crashed through a soldier's tent. After that incident, Major Earl Long of the marine contingent set out to find a suitable alternate site for a landing field on the tableland of Jones Mountain. That idea was given up only when Major Long and Joe Fray encountered broken trees and limbs on the Jones Mountain Trail blocking their passage by horseback when they climbed the mountain to inspect the site.

In due course, the mountain people adjusted to the Hoover entourage, but the wild hogs and some of the domestic stock did not fare as well. Hoover's kitchen crew gave the presidential garbage to Ben Shifflett, who fed it to his hogs, apparently with disastrous results. The animals contracted hog cholera, an infectious disease that spread to the wild hog population and some of the domestic animals in the Jones Mountain area. That year, Will Shifflett butchered and sold fifty domestic hogs to clear his pens before the disease affected the stock.

In the year 1930, a forest fire swept up Big Kinsey Hollow and raged out of control across Jones Mountain. Valley farmers fought the blaze for twenty-seven days before extinguishing it. "That fire just kept burning," Johnnie Shifflett said. "We'd put it out, and it would burn through the dry ivy [laurel] roots and come out again a hundred feet away. We dug a fire line across there and finally got the fire stopped." The fire destroyed vegetation across the south face of the mountain, down the Wilson Run side stream, and across the mountain to the head of McDaniel Hollow. The Staunton River Valley and the area around Bear Church escaped damage.

After President Hoover lost the election in 1932, he deeded the Rapidan Camp as a gift to the government for the new national park. For a while, the camp was used by cabinet members and later by Boy Scouts. The Civilian Conservation Corps constructed a new circuit trail from Hoover's cabinet camp (lower on the Rapidan) to the summit of Doubletop. They also constructed a footpath along the crest of Fork Mountain from the new road to Piney Knob, behind the Shifflett and Gallehugh houses.

On September 15, 1934, Skyline Drive was opened at Big Meadows and along the west side of Hazeltop Ridge, about two miles from Laurel Gap. Within one year, a half million visitors drove up the mountain parkway in 150,000 automobiles.

Part II

The Lord of the Mountain

When the sun is in the sky,
And the heat waves are on high,
And my barley fields are dry,
I'm not afraid.
When the sun is hid away night and day,
Day after day,
And the drenching clouds hold sway,
I'm not afraid.
I'm not afraid of flood by night.
I'm not afraid of drought by day.
Or nature's smiles, her wiles, her guiles,
Her errant way, her frightening might,
I'm not afraid.
Rain, sunshine—sun and shade,
That is how my crops are made.
Every stalk and every blade.
I'm not afraid.
My barley's in the shed.
My corn's in the bin.
The hay's in place.
My animals are fed.
And by God's grace,
I'm not afraid.

"And by God's Grace"
A poem about Buck Hawkins
by Edward A. Bacon

Harvey loaded the last of his belongings into a large wooden box and carried it out into the yard. He stood silently for a long time beside the cabin, where he had known the joys and sorrows of a full life. Then he hoisted the box to his shoulder and walked slowly down to the stream, near a trailhead below his hog pen. He paused there for another moment and looked back, then trudged wearily down the trail. It was Harvey's last walk on a trail that he had hiked for seventy years.

That day in the spring of 1937 was like the ending of a dynasty. Harvey Nichols put his Jones Mountain Cabin behind him as the new Shenandoah National park took over his land. It was land that had been in the Nichols family for nearly ninety years.

The Nichols Family

The Nichols family—known then by the name Nicholson—came from North Carolina about 1820 and settled on the south side of Bluff Mountain, in the rugged Conway River Valley. The early homesite was on a flat at the base of a rocky bluff, just north of the Haunted Branch. The land eventually became part of the Jarrell place, occupied by George Jarrell and his wife, the former Susan McDaniel. They left about 1920, and by 1930 the original Nicholson buildings had collapsed. The land was later to be acquired by the government for the Rapidan Wildlife Management Area. The adjacent land near the Devils Ditch became part of the Shenandoah National Park.

One branch of the Nicholson family left the Conway River in August of 1848 and settled on 120 acres of land on the rough eastern spine of Jones Mountain below the Rock Church. The land included some forested promontories, a mountain spring back in a hollow below a flat, and the famous Rock Church itself. The area included the site of the present-day Jones Mountain Cabin.

David "Davey" Nicholson purchased the land from Philander Goodall for a price of 400 bushels of rye, payable to Goodall in five annual installments of eighty bushels each. In the event of a crop failure, Davey Nicholson was to pay $40 in place of the installment of rye.

Davey and his wife Mary and their eight children lived at the site from 1848 until 1854. Then the land was deeded to twenty-two-year-old Pleasant Nicholson and his twenty-year-old brother Albert Nicholson, nephews of Davey and sons of Alexander and Sarah Nicholson of the Conway Valley. The signing of the deed was witnessed by Robert A. Banks, the man destined to become a general in the Confederate States Army. Banks, in fact, was more than a witness, since he held a mortgage to the land. Later, the mortgage was paid off, and the Jones Mountain tract was transferred with full title to the Nicholson brothers.

For three years, from 1854 until 1857, Pleasant and his wife Betsy Ann lived on the tract. In 1857, they sold their half interest to Albert Nicholson, who became the sole owner of the tract. In the mid-1850s, Albert had courted and then married Maria Catherine Estes of Graves Mill. She was known as Kitty. Their daughter Comora was born in 1857, when Kitty was twenty-one.

About this time, the family changed their name to Nichols (sometimes spelled Nichol and Nicol). Some evidence indicates that the family had never used the name Nicholson, although that was the name used in the various land deeds and the official records of the U.S. Census. In later years, Albert Nichols filed a correction in the county land records.

In the meantime, about 1855, Albert constructed a cabin near the spring and lived there with Kitty and Comoro during the years before and after the Civil War. The stone foundation and the enormous chimney that Albert Nichols built are the same as those of the present-day Jones Mountain Cabin in Shenandoah National Park. The present restored structure is almost a duplicate of Albert Nichols' early cabin. The original cabin was fifteen by twenty-two feet, with two floors and an attic. The first floor was actually a basement with a front door at the ground level. A roofed deck in front of the cabin at the second, or main floor, level extended the full length of the structure, similar to but longer than the porch on the present-day cabin. Steps led up to the porch deck. There was a ground-level rear door on the main floor. The original building had fireplaces both in the basement and on the main floor.

It was peaceful on the mountain until uneasiness spread about the threat of civil war. Then, following the secession of Virginia, Albert Nichols was mustered into the new Confederate States Army. He was assigned in May of 1861 to Letcher's Battery, Pegram's Battalion, in the

Army of Northern Virginia, under the command of Captain Greenlee Davidson.

At the end of the war in 1865, Albert returned to his home on Jones Mountain. There, he and Kitty continued to rear a family, eventually numbering ten children. Their first son, Harvey Walker Nichols, was born at the Jones Mountain Cabin in 1866. As a boy, Harvey Nichols spent much of his time exploring the mountains around the Rock Church and the Staunton River.

In the 1870s, Albert and Kitty moved to the Graves Mill Valley below the south flank of Jones Mountain, where they rented an eighty-acre farm. In 1876, they purchased the farm from Francis E. Graves, then acquired another 150 acres on Jones (Kinsey) Run, adjacent to the farm. For several years, the family lived in a long log building that had been the slave church before the Civil War. Later, Albert Nichols constructed a larger log house closer to Jones Mountain.

Daughter Comora Nichols grew up to become an attractive young woman. When she was twenty-one, she returned from the Graves Mill Valley to the mountains as the bride of John L. Jenkins. About 1886, son Harvey Nichols, who was still lured by the spell of Jones Mountain, returned to the Jones Mountain Cabin below Bear Church. There he lived for the next fifty years.

All that remains of the old Nicholson (or Nichols) place on the Conway River. The cabin collapsed in the 1930s.

Albert Nichols, builder of the original Jones Mountain Cabin, sitting with his wife Kitty and seven of their children outside their home near Graves Mill. Two daughters, seated, are unidentified. Back row, left to right, Wood, Carrie, Harvey, Mary Lou, and an unidentified daughter. Log building with chimney was a slave church before the Civil War. Photo was made about 1888. Photo in 1979 (below) was taken at the same site. Note large stone in lower center of each picture.

Harvey Nichols

Harvey Walker Nichols was built like a bull, thickset and muscular, with broad shoulders, five feet eight inches tall, his weight ranging from 180 to 200 pounds. His dark brown hair was thin and receding. In the years after he returned to Jones Mountain, Harvey wore a bull-horn mustache, sometimes curled at the ends. He usually wore a big black hat. He spoke in a deep baritone voice.

"Harvey was an honest man," Charles Jenkins said. "And he had a good sense of humor. People liked him, but some of his relatives and the church people were down on him because he drank liquor and ran around with women."

Harvey was fairly well educated, a rare circumstance in the mountains in those years. Some of his education was traceable to his teen-age years in the Graves Mill Valley, where schooling was available, but evidence suggests that he was largely self-educated. "Harvey was a smart man," Dewey Shifflett said.

Harvey had powerful arms and legs. "Harvey Nichols was the strongest man that ever lived in these mountains," Elton Berry said. "We were working on the road one day when Harvey came by. He had been to the store and he was walking back to his cabin. He was carrying a bag of groceries with his right hand and holding onto a bag of corn meal and a bag of flour that were slung over his left shoulder. He was carrying a can of coal oil with his left hand. And he stopped and talked to us for a solid hour without putting any of that down. The bag of meal by itself weighed over fifty pounds. He did that all the time, and he carried those loads right up that steep trail below his cabin."

Neighbor Hume Lillard agreed. "I saw Harvey pick up a big wooden barrel, one of those barrels they used to keep soda pop in. Harvey picked up that barrel and put it on his shoulder and carried it right up that mountain."

Harvey needed the barrel to use as a mash barrel for his distillery. "He made liquor up there, you know," Lillard said.

Harvey's principal livelihood for nearly sixty years was moonshining: distilling and selling liquor without a license. He made rye whiskey and apple brandy and occasionally peach and blackberry brandy. He grew his own grain and fruit, although he sometimes purchased rye at Graves Mill. His whiskey was known as Harvey's Special, noted for its smooth, mellow taste.

"The better-to-do people bought from Harvey because his whiskey was good," Charles Jenkins said. "His whiskey was clean. A lot of whiskey in those days was not clean, but Harvey was proud of his whiskey. He kept the copper and the glass clean. Harvey's Special was a lot better than what you get off the shelf today. He made good whiskey. I tasted quite a bit of it myself.''

Harvey kept his still chained to a tree near the springhouse. He bottled and sold the liquor in fruit jars, jugs, and kegs ranging in size from one pint to ten gallons.

Harvey Nichols' reputation for high quality whiskey and brandy brought customers from throughout Madison County. Most of the buyers climbed the mountain, but occasionally Harvey met customers at prearranged locations, usually at the grist mill at Graves Mill. He usually

Harvey Nichols, about 1886.

charged twenty-five cents for a pint of whiskey and fifty cents for a half gallon of brandy.

Harvey enjoyed drinking his own Harvey's Special, and he handled it well. "I never once saw Harvey Nichols drunk," James McDaniel said.

Harvey was much more than a moonshiner. He led an active life as a farmer, a sportsman, a hiker, and, after he married, a family man. He understood horses and cattle. He knew the land and the crops. And he was wise in the ways of people.

"Harvey made liquor, sure, but he was a farmer," Homer Shifflett said, objecting to branding Harvey as just another moonshiner. "He was a good farmer. He knew how to raise crops. My God, I suppose he was good—he lived up there fifty years raising crops. A lot of people tried that and didn't make it. Hell, Harvey was a good farmer."

Besides rye, peaches, and apples, Harvey grew subsistence crops and a vegetable garden. He cultivated the garden with two horses named Daisy and Kit and later a mule named Old Dan. The garden and a small vineyard were located in front of the cabin. An orchard with sixty-two apple trees was below the garden. Harvey grew beans, corn, and rye in fields on the promontory beyond the springhouse, on the flat above the cabin, and in the ravine behind the cabin. A hog pen was below the spring. A barn was located in the ravine, and two animal sheds were on a hillside between the cabin and the flat. About 85 acres of the 120-acre tract were forested.

Harvey kept hogs, sheep, chickens, and two cows. Milk and eggs were refrigerated in the springhouse, where a pool of water was fed by the cold mountain spring. Dried beans and sugar-cured ham hung in the attic of the cabin.

During the years from 1886 to 1897, Harvey apparently lived alone at the Jones Mountain Cabin. During this period, he gained a reputation as a woman's man and spent much of his time hiking the trails to distant hollows, where he visited pretty girls. "The girls visited Harvey too," Charles Jenkins said.

Harvey traveled once all the way to Washington, D.C., reportedly to see pretty girls. He and his brother Wood (George Gatewood Nichols) made the long trip in a new buggy that Wood had purchased, drawn by one of the Nichols horses. As they arrived in the capital, Harvey and Wood eagerly anticipated the sights of the city, but the horse, trained only for the mountains and fields, became increasingly nervous. Suddenly, it bolted.

"That horse ran off down the street and tore up that new buggy, and I don't know how they got back to the mountains," Harvey's son Nick said.

Harvey and Eula

Harvey, in due time, settled down to serious living and became a devoted husband. In his hikes across the mountains, he eventually found his way beyond Big Meadows to Tanners Ridge and down into the remote Pine Grove Hollow. There, in the late 1890s, he met and courted Eula Lea Yowell, a woman six years younger than himself. They were married in Page County on May 29, 1899.

It wasn't long before Eula Nichols settled into her new life on Jones Mountain. She cooked the meals, kept the cabin clean, and helped with farm chores. "People liked Eula," recalled Dewey Shifflett, who knew her when he was a teen-ager growing up in the Staunton River Valley. "Eula was a gentle person, nice and kind. She talked friendly to us, and she had a sense of humor about everything."

Harvey worked the orchard and fields and tilled the garden. He cut and stacked firewood. At harvest time, he cradled and cured rye, shocked it into bundles, threshed it by hand, and carried the grain to the grist mill. In the winter, he forked silage to the cows and fed corn to the hogs.

In 1900, they had their first child, Maude, born in the Jones Mountain Cabin. Three other daughters, Edna, Alice, and Minnie, were born between 1903 and 1910. The Jones Mountain Cabin was vibrant with the activity of a young and growing family.

But the birth of Minnie in 1910 brought serious medical problems, and Eula was taken by wagon to a hospital in Charlottesville. She recovered, but two years later, during the attempted delivery of a fifth child, her condition worsened. It was too late to get her to a doctor. Harvey could not save his wife, and she died during childbirth at the Jones Mountain Cabin. She was thirty-nine. The baby was also lost.

On the day of Eula's burial in 1912, Melvin and Dewey Shifflett and several other pallbearers carried the coffin up the steep slope behind the cabin, then across the flat and down the mountain on the switchback trail. Grim-faced Harvey Nichols and several family friends walked behind with the children. "It was a long way to the cemetery. There were several of us as pallbearers, and we took turns," Dewey Shifflett said.

At the bottom of the mountain, they passed through a hollow, then walked slowly across Bush Field toward the distant hillside cemetery beside a grove of trees near the Staunton River. About seventy-five people waited there in silence as the pallbearers approached.

At the graveside, the Reverend Mr. Carter of Graves Chapel spoke for about fifteen minutes. Then they buried Eula Lea Nichols near a separate grove of trees off to the side, about fifty feet from the other graves. "That was such a beautiful place," Effie McDaniel recalled. "It was next to the trees beside a beautiful green field."

On Christmas Eve of that same year, the patriarch Albert Nichols, builder of the original Jones Mountain Cabin, died at Graves Mill. He was seventy-nine. In his will, he bequeathed to his son Harvey a lifetime estate in the 120-acre Jones Mountain land. Harvey thereupon became the seventeenth owner of the land since 1660.

Eula Lea Nichols, first wife of Harvey Nichols. Photo was made about 1905. Original picture has been retouched.

Life at the Jones Mountain Cabin

Following the death of Eula, Harvey was left with the responsibility of rearing the four daughters. Maude, the oldest, was then only twelve. Housekeeping was not new to Harvey, since he had lived alone for several years before he married Eula.

They cooked and ate on the ground floor. "Harvey was a good cook," recalled Johnnie Shifflett, who sometimes ate with the family.

At each meal, including breakfast, Harvey drank a glass of Harvey's Special whiskey mixed with water and sugar, a drink that he called a hot pot. He made the drinks strong, one part whiskey to one part water. He required each child to take one spoonful.

"We had plenty to eat," daughter Minnie said. "We had hot bread three times a day. Pappa gave us heavy bread and gravy for breakfast. For dinner and supper, we usually had beans, cabbage, and fried potatoes. We had our own cured ham, but we also ate coon, squirrel, possum, and ground hog. We had all the milk we wanted.

"Sometimes, Pappa got up early in the morning before the sun was up, and he went down to the Run [Staunton River] and he brought back a mess of fish, and we'd have fresh trout and beans for breakfast.

"Pappa knew how to preserve food. He dug a hole and laid down straw, and buried cabbage, potatoes, and apples. They lasted all year. We ate green beans in the summer and snap beans in the winter. We had potatoes year round. We butchered hogs and cured the bacon, sausage, and shoulder. We grew corn and ground it into meal down at the mill. We bought sugar and coffee and flour."

As the girls grew, Harvey put them to work keeping house, milking cows, and doing other farm chores. They also had time for recreation, of which their favorite activity was riding horses on the Jones Mountain trails. The children acquired a basic education, although they attended the school at Graves Mill only a year or two. Most of their learning was acquired in the home. They were exceptionally intelligent children. "They were pretty too," recalled Rosetta Lamb. "They were as pretty as they could be."

On the long summer days, the family retired to bed when darkness fell, then rose at the first light of dawn. "We went to sleep with the chickens and got up with the chickens," Minnie said. In the winters they stayed up late, often sitting together near the fireplace. The rooms were lighted by kerosene lamps.

Harvey slept on the ground floor on a large bed located at the end of the room opposite the fireplace. Sometimes he slept sitting in a chair near the fire. He was a light sleeper. "If a cat walked across the room, Pappa would wake up," said one of the daughters. The girls usually slept on the second, or main, floor, but on stormy nights when strong winds rattled the windows and rafters, they went to the basement until the storm passed.

Harvey Nichols was a disciplinarian, often impatient with his daughters. "Pappa beat us. He was mean," said Minnie, still out of temper sixty years later. "Maude was a young woman, and she wanted nice dresses. So she took some of our meat down to the store at Graves Mill and traded it for some clothes, and I never saw a horse get a whippin' like Maude got. Pappa used hickory."

But even Minnie admitted that sometimes the girls were mischievous. One icy winter day when Harvey was away, Maude let the sheep out of the shed to see how well the animals could walk on the solid ice that covered Jones Mountain. "The sheep started slipping and falling and rolling down through the orchard and on down the steep trail. They kept going, and they slid all the way down to the Run at the bottom of the mountain. Maude got a whippin' for that."

Sometimes Harvey mixed humor with the punishment. On one dark, moonless night he punished young Minnie by making her sleep outside. She became frightened in the darkness and huddled with the dogs near the basement window, which Harvey called the dog coop. "I was laying there with the dogs, and a big black thing crawled up over a boulder near the window and started growling," Minnie said. "It was Pappa trying to scare me."

Harvey Nichols was an ardent outdoorsman who spent much of his time hunting, fishing, and walking. He also maintained a network of trails that went out from the cabin and the crest of Jones Mountain.

Harvey liked to fish in bad weather. He often left the cabin in the gray mist of dawn and fished for wild trout in the boulder-strewn middle section of the Staunton River. He seldom used a pole, preferring to work the line with his hands. Harvey always caught fish, often pulling in ten-inch brook trout, using red worms as bait.

For hunting, Harvey had a pistol and a twelve-gauge shotgun. He hunted squirrels during the days but preferred night hunting, when he went after coon and possum. "Harvey was a great night hunter. He always got coon. He always brought back fresh meat," Dewey Shifflett said.

"Sometimes, we practically lived on coon," Minnie added. "I hated it."

Harvey frequently hunted alone, but sometimes he took one of his daughters and often hunted with Will Shifflett or one of the Shifflett boys. The hunts usually lasted all night and customarily followed the same trails. From the upper cabin trail he went down the present-day McDaniel Hollow Trail, up through the hemlock Wilderness to the Adam Hurt Field near the Sag, then to the top of Jones Mountain, back along the Jones Mountain Trail to the rock ridge, and back down to the cabin, a distance of about eight miles, not counting side trips in search of game. He usually bypassed Cat Knob, taking the old short-cut trail that the pioneers had constructed along the contours of Little Cat Knob. He also customarily bypassed Bear Church, passing down across the hollows to the cabin. Occasionally, Harvey forayed to Fork Mountain from Hundleys Ford or climbed up Johnsons Ground or Back Field Hollow to the top of Jones Mountain.

Harvey's hunting dogs did all the work, ranging ahead to pick up scent. When the dogs got too far afield, Harvey signaled them back by blowing a cow's horn which he carried on a shoulder strap. "In the middle of the night, when we woke up and heard a cow's horn, we knew Harvey was up there in the mountains," Dewey Shifflett said.

Daughter Minnie frequently hunted with her father. "We'd leave after dark," she remembered. "Pappa carried a lantern and a shotgun and an ax, and I followed behind in the dark. When the dogs treed a coon and started barking, we'd hurry and catch up. Pappa chopped down the tree, and the dogs caught the coon. We went all night, way back across the mountains, and we got back about daybreak."

Harvey enjoyed hiking, and he spent much of his time cutting back the brush and overhanging branches on the eight-mile circuit trail and five trails that went out from the cabin.

"Pappa was a walker. My God, he was a walker!" said Minnie. Harvey hiked the Cat Knob circuit several hundred times. He walked to Graves Mill more than two thousand times, usually down and up a steep ravine near the Lillard Distillery. He tramped the trails many times while en route to see friends in the Staunton Valley and distant places such as Doubletop and the Devils Ditch.

And when he was again a single man in the years after 1912, Harvey once more took to the trails to find girls.

"According to the Bible," Harvey said, "every man is supposed to have seven women hanging onto his coattail, and I hope I live long enough to have seven women hanging onto mine."

Harvey was drawn to young women, although he was now approaching fifty himself. Eventually, he returned to the hollow below Tanners Ridge, where he met Sheed, a beautiful young woman who was sought after by the men of the mountains. Every week for almost a year, Harvey walked fifteen miles across the mountains to the hollow. Most of the trips lasted half the week, since one day was required going and another returning, and Harvey stayed in the hollow one or two days each trip.

When Harvey made his trips to the hollow, he sometimes farmed out his daughters and the dogs to the Shiffletts or the Breedens, although occasionally he left them in the charge of Maude, the oldest daughter.

The trails which Harvey followed to Pine Grove were the same as those he hiked in the 1890s when he courted Eula. He usually proceeded along the McDaniel Hollow Trail, then up through the Wilderness to the Sag, and down what is now the Fork Mountain Trail. From the Laurel Prong, Harvey climbed directly to Milam Gap on a now-abandoned grade, then followed an old road (approximately the route of the present-day Appalachian Trail) to Tanners Ridge, and climbed down Fronk's path on the west side of the Blue Ridge. Sometimes, Harvey went or returned on a different route. He dropped down to Bush Field on the switchback trail, crossed Fork Mountain on the Shifflett footpath, then proceeded up the rough buggy trail to Big Meadows and on to Tanners Ridge. About 85 percent of the trails are now within Shenandoah National Park.

The courtship with Sheed went on for about fifty trips. Social gossip about Harvey's success and popularity spread through the mountains. But for all the times Harvey went to the hollow, Sheed seldom returned the visits by going to Bear Church, and eventually the relationship ended.

Harvey Nichols was never in the doldrums for long. He preferred cheer and happiness, and neighbors said he was always ready to help people in need. In 1918, he had that opportunity when a major epidemic of influenza struck half the population of the area and killed several people. Harvey spent many days visiting the sick in mountain homes. He cooked for the families, did the chores, and ran errands. Harvey beat the disease himself by drinking extra whiskey and carrying an onion in his pocket.

"Harvey was a good man," Charles Jenkins said. "He was honest, and once he got to know you, he'd do anything for you."

The Fire

The year 1918 was to be remembered by most people as the year when the troops came marching home from the World War. For Harvey Nichols, it was to be remembered as the year when his Jones Mountain Cabin burned to the ground.

It was a warm day in the early spring of the year, about the first of May. The sheep had wandered off, as they often did, and Harvey and the girls went out to locate them. They found the sheep down by the Run in Bush Field and herded them back up the switchback trail.

Near the top, Harvey saw smoke and hastened on. Mounting the crest of the ridge, he looked down in horror to see the sixty-year-old Jones Mountain Cabin in a ball of fire.

Harvey screamed, each word a prolonged, mournful cry:

"Oh—my—God!" It was a scream that daughter Minnie would never forget.

Down in the Staunton Valley, Will Shifflett and his boys were planting corn on the mountainside when the horses whinnied and stomped and Will looked up to see smoke billowing from the mountain below Bear Church.

"Harvey's house is on fire!" he yelled.

The younger boys held the horses as Will and the older boys ran down to the Staunton River, then bounded up the mountain, staggered across the flat, and stood helplessly beside Harvey Nichols.

There was nothing they could do but stand and watch. The roof caved in and then the walls. All of the Nichols' belongings went up in smoke: their furniture and clothing, personal items, the meat in the attic, the family Bible . . . .

Harvey Nichols never knew what started the fire. It was years later when Minnie found out that the fire resulted from the reckless act of a juvenile. Minnie understood and forgave, but she knew better than to tell her father. "One fire will ruin a man," Harvey had told his daughters.

Harvey moved temporarily into an animal shed above the cabin site. Minnie was taken in by the Breedens, whose daughter Effie was six years older. Edna, Alice, and Maude were taken by the Shiffletts, who had children the same ages.

Harvey worked for several months during the summer and autumn of 1918 building a new Jones Mountain Cabin on the same foundation and with the same chimney as the old. He dressed the rock seams with mud and clay. He felled chestnut trees from the upper forest and pulled them by horse to the cabin site. Harvey worked as diligently as a craftsman, scoring and hewing the timbers and notching them to fit. He also hewed the shingles for the roof. He worked mostly alone but sometimes had help late in the days from friends Will Shifflett and Wilmer Jenkins. One by one the logs were hoisted and fitted and the seams filled with clay. Next, he built the roof.

Dewey Shifflett and Kenny McDaniel hauled lumber by wagon from Kite's Sawmill below Graves Mill. "My God," Dewey recalled, "that road up to Harvey's cabin was rocky and steep! It was a son-of-gun place to get to with horses and a wagon."

Harvey completed the frames for the doors and windows, then nailed weather boarding to the logs to provide insulation and protect the logs from the elements. He did not paint the cabin.

The new Jones Mountain Cabin was only slightly changed from the old one. The new structure did not have a porch or a ground-level entrance on the second floor. Harvey closed off the upper fireplace. The basement became the main floor, where the wood flooring was laid directly on the ground, a building technique that was commonly used during the years of the log cabin when rot-resistant chestnut lumber was plentiful.

After Harvey finished his new cabin in the fall of 1918, he set about the job of making tables, chairs, and benches for the new home. Neighbors gave him a housewarming and donated several items including beds, kitchen utensils, and a dish safe. Then, with the furniture in place and his daughters back home, Harvey turned his thoughts to some important business that had been neglected too long.

Prohibition

Harvey Nichols' preoccupation with the cabin in 1918 diverted his attention from the enactment of prohibition in Virginia a year earlier, specifically outlawing the manufacture and sale of alcoholic beverages. All of the bonded distilleries in the area closed, including the Lillard Distillery on the Staunton River. The shortage of whiskey and brandy beginning in 1918 substantially increased the demand for moonshine products. As a result, production increased.

"You could go to Jones Mountain and get apple brandy faster than you could get a glass of water," rancher Bob Smith said.

The price of good whiskey increased, and the best whiskey in the mountain area was Harvey's Special, the rye whiskey made popular by the simple virtue of cleanliness: whiskey drawn from clean copper and aged in clean kegs. The man who had been creating this great whiskey without a license since the 1800's now became one of the better known men among an important segment of the population of Madison County. Business had always been good for Harvey Nichols, and now his mellow whiskey drew the attention of some of the finest citizens of the county, including politicians and businessmen.

"Harvey Nichols made enough liquor that you could swim in it all the way to Graves Mill," said farmer Frank Jarrell. And to maintain this level of business, Harvey had to stay one step ahead of the law.

To avoid apprehension by government agents, Harvey often carried the equipment to a small creek in another hollow on his land, reached by a trail beyond the springhouse. Maude stood watch at the cabin, with instructions from her father to fire the shotgun as a signal if any strangers appeared.

Maude knew how to use a shotgun, having fired it many times when Harvey was off courting at Pine Grove. Then one day the opportunity came to fire for real, when Harvey was working his still in the other hollow and two strangers came down the trail to the cabin.

103

"Maude didn't just fire a signal. She fired right at those men. And those men turned and ran, and we never saw them again," Minnie said.

Also as a means of avoiding apprehension, Harvey stored the liquor in kegs at hidden locations in the surrounding woods. He once even enlisted the help of Assistant County Treasurer (later Treasurer) Joe Fray to transport a keg on horseback to a location in the woods. Dressed in an army officer's uniform from the World War, Fray rode a young mare up to Harvey's cabin early one Monday morning. It was his first meeting with the moonshiner. Fray was accompanied by Will Shifflett.

Harvey came out of the cabin and immediately suspected the man in the uniform. "Boy, who are you?" Harvey asked the thirty-two year old Fray. Joe Fray introduced himself.

Harvey was still cautious. He didn't like the uniform. "You speak with a smooth tongue, boy. What do you want?" "Joe's okay, Harvey. He's a good man," Will Shifflett said.

"Well, then, get down off that horse and come in," Harvey said. Inside, Harvey poured apple brandy into a jelly glass and handed it to Joe Fray. "Have a drink, boy."

Joe was in good spirits when he left. He purchased a quart of brandy and then helped Harvey move a keg of whiskey into the woods above the cabin. With Harvey leading the way on foot, Joe rode the mare, trying to hold onto the five-gallon keg. The saddle was loose, and the tipsy Joe started wobbling and weaving. Several times, the county official nearly fell off the horse, but Harvey eventually got him to the destination.

At least one tipsy customer did fall off a horse after stopping at Harvey's. A respected member of a prominent political family, the man was one of Harvey Nichols' best friends and a valued customer. He always rode his horse up to the cabin to buy whiskey and usually stayed for a drink. One time, after a few drinks, the customer decided to buy a ten-gallon jug of Harvey's Special and carry it down the trail on horseback. He made it up to the flat and started down the switchback trail toward Bush Field. But at the first steep switchback, he toppled over the front of the horse and flipflopped to the ground. The jug broke, and ten gallons of good whiskey splashed like a wave and washed on down the path.

Harvey and Cricket

Back in the early 1800s, a trail was constructed down the southwest side of Jones Mountain to Bootens Run and the upper Conway River. The early pioneers of the Conway Valley had used it for passage across the mountain to Johnsons Ground and the Staunton River and as a link to the high Sugar Hollow Trail. In 1920, more than a hundred years later,

Harvey Nichols scrambled down the trail on his way to the distant Devils Ditch, where he visited and courted Mary Susan "Cricket" Taylor, beautiful daughter of Mat and Rosa Taylor. Their cabin was located about two miles up the rugged Devils Ditch Hollow, not far from the present-day Bearfence Mountain Shelter in Shenandoah National Park.

"Cricket was the prettiest girl who ever walked the Middle River," said Sevilla Powell.

Twenty-four years old with velvet black hair and piercing dark eyes, Cricket was a radiant but reserved person. Her emotions were seldom ruffled. "She didn't talk too much, but she was friendly," Homer Shifflett said.

"Cricket was a popular person," Nick Nichols said. "Everyone thought the world of her."

The courting lasted several weeks. Then Harvey, fifty-four years old and eager to have a new wife, pulled off one of the great romantic triumphs of the mountains when he persuaded Cricket to come to Jones Mountain. "Pappa told us we were going to have a housekeeper," Minnie said.

At the Jones Mountain Cabin, Cricket worked all day cooking, keeping house, mending clothes, and helping to supervise the three youngest daughters, then aged ten to seventeen. She helped Harvey rebuild and extend some split-rail fences around the fields. She also walked with him to Graves Mill to get groceries, clothing, and other supplies. Usually they did not linger at the store, where friends gathered to visit, but preferred to return to the mountain.

Cricket was a talented banjo player, although she did not read music. In the summer evenings of 1921, she often sat in front of the cabin playing the songs and ballads of the mountains. People gathered to listen. And on cold winter nights she played the banjo while sitting at the fireside.

Time passed, and Harvey announced that Cricket was expecting a child. As the day approached, Cricket's mother, Rosa Taylor, came from the Devils Ditch to attend the delivery at the cabin. Neighbor Lucy Breeden came up from the Staunton River to help.

It was June of 1922. The day was hot. That night, Cricket gave birth to twins, a boy and a girl. But the young woman was stricken and died just after the childbirth. "That night at the cabin was a terrible night, the worst suffering that I have ever witnessed," Minnie Nichols said.

Harvey Nichols was torn deeply by grief. He selected a burial site beside a peach tree on the open flat above the cabin. He wanted Cricket's grave to be close by. Fat Breeden brought a coffin up the mountain by wagon from Wolftown. On the day of the burial, the neighbors and

Cricket Taylor (standing) and Eliza Roach at the St. Andrews-on-the-Mountain Mission, November 1916. The mission was on Roach Mountain (known today as Cliff Mountain) near the present-day Bear Fence Mountain Shelter in Shenandoah National Park about a thousand feet from what is now Skyline Drive. The photo was probably made by Episcopal missionary Carrie Makley, who wrote in her diary that Cricket stayed overnight at the mission on November 16-17, 1916. On November 20, Makley wrote, "Cricket came to help us peel apples till midnight." This was about the time of Cricket's 21st birthday.

relatives from the mountains around Graves Mill and the Devils Ditch gathered on the Jones Mountain flat.

"All of us on the Wilson Run and the Rapidan went up for the burial service. There was a right smart crowd up there that day," Effie McDaniel said. They buried Cricket beside the peach tree at the site Harvey selected. The grave was marked by two fieldstones. In later years, Harvey maintained a wood fence around the plot.

The Lonely Years

One by one, Harvey's daughters grew up and left Jones Mountain. Minnie, the last to depart, left in 1925, when she was fifteen years old. After that, Harvey Nichols once again lived alone on the mountain. He was now approaching the age of sixty.

Up at sunrise every morning, he continued to farm the land, feed the animals, and operate his still. He worked in the garden and cultivated rosebushes and spirea, which he grew near the cabin. He cooked his meals, washed the dishes, and kept his cabin immaculately clean. Late in the days, he often sat in front of the cabin and gazed down beyond the cleared fields and orchards to the distant valleys and ridges.

Friend Cleve Cave of Pine Grove often visited, sometimes staying several days at a time. In the evenings after supper, Will Shifflett and his sons occasionally came up the mountain to visit. After dark, they got out a deck of cards and played pitch or sitback by the light of a kerosene lamp.

Harvey also continued to hunt and fish, now usually going alone to ply the waters or roam the mountains at night. He spent a lot of time with his four dogs, especially Nina, his favorite hunting dog. "Harvey minded his own business. He left everyone else alone," Dewey Shifflett said.

Harvey walked to Graves Mill about once a week and occasionally rode his mule, Old Dan. Charles Jenkins recalled that even when Harvey rode the mule he still carried the large sacks of cornmeal over his shoulder. "Keeps the horsehair out of the cornmeal," Harvey said, a glint of humor in his eyes.

Harvey never lost his sense of humor. A roan bull strayed from the Landrum cattle herd at Big Meadows and for several months roamed the flats on Fork Mountain, occasionally coming down to the orchards to eat apples. Harvey had seen signs of the animal on his hikes across the mountains and told friends that an "elk" was running wild. Then one Sunday morning when snow was on the ground, Harvey organized an elk hunt. Sidney Fray, Field Kite, and Charles Jenkins showed up at Hundleys Ford with their horses, hunting dogs, and rifles.

"You men wait here, and I'll circle back with the hounds and run the elk down this way," Harvey said.

The men waited while Harvey hustled up into the Wilderness with the dogs. Sometime later, the roan bull came charging down the Staunton River trail, the dogs yelping at his feet.

Everyone laughed. Harvey was having a good time, and now he suggested that they run the animal down to Graves Chapel and into the church, where the Sunday morning service was then in session. They stopped short of that, but everyone had another good laugh.

In 1929, when President Herbert Hoover built his summer White House on the nearby Laurel Prong, life went on about the same for Harvey Nichols. During the construction of several new roads and trails for the president's party, Harvey scrambled across the mountain to meet and talk with the work crews. Later, army sentries blocked passage on many of the trails, but late at night Harvey continued to prowl the woods with his lantern in search of game, sometimes passing within a mile of the summer White House. During the days, presidential guests crossed the same area riding horses to the observation tower on Fork Mountain.

In due course, modern transportation came to Graves Mill, and at the age of sixty-five, Harvey Nichols learned to drive the automobile. Later, he purchased a brand new car, a shiny green 1933 Hudson. Since Harvey could not bring the car even close to the cabin, he chained it to a tree near Graves Mill. For about a year, he occasionally drove the vehicle on the country roads, usually to the county seat at Madison. Then trouble developed in the master cylinder, which Harvey called the brake box. After that, he let the car sit. He apparently preferred riding Old Dan or walking, and for several years he left the car in a shed behind Elmo Utz's store in Graves Mill. Eventually, he sold it.

Harvey and Lady

After a few years, Harvey tired of living alone and again set out on the mountain trails to find companionship. "In those years, Harvey was just a damned stray cat," Charles Jenkins said. "He was always turning up in some hollow five or ten miles away."

But Harvey knew what he was doing, and his wanderings rewarded him richly. He returned often to the Devils Ditch, where he courted Lady Taylor, a younger sister of Cricket. Again, Harvey became the envy of the mountain men, when he prevailed upon the thirty-three-year-old woman to become his wife and move to Jones Mountain. Harvey was sixty-seven.

"Lady was a very good looking woman with a right nice figure," Charles Jenkins said. She was of medium height with dark brown hair and had the discernible features of her part-Indian ancestry: the sharp face and the dark, penetrating eyes.

Lady frequently walked the roads and trails, usually on the way to Graves Mill for provisions. "She always wore hightop boots," recalled Dolly Hawkins Seekford, daughter of Buck Hawkins.

Lady and Harvey both liked music. Harvey purchased a wind-up Victrola phonograph and a collection of records, mostly hymns and country music. Lady especially liked the sad but romantic mountain ballad "Maple on the Hill," which she listened to on the Victrola and sometimes played on the banjo. Harvey's favorite song was "The Star-Spangled Banner." In those years the national anthem blared frequently from the phonograph in the Jones Mountain Cabin.

Harvey and Lady both liked old-time hymns. One time, when friend Wilmer Jenkins stopped at the cabin to visit, Harvey and Lady were listening to the hymn "How Beautiful Heaven Must Be."

"Oh, that's a beautiful song," Lady said. "Play it again, Harvey. Heaven must be beautiful!"

"Yeah, but gettin' thar!" Harvey said. Getting there was something else. He looked at Lady and they laughed.

Those were joyful years for Harvey and Lady. Perhaps the best year was 1935. On the night of June 29, while a storm raged outside, Lady gave birth to a son at the Jones Mountain Cabin. Lady's mother Rosa hiked up from the Devils Ditch to attend the birth as the midwife, assisted by Minnie and Alice, who had come home to help their father. They worked by the light of a kerosene lamp. Lightning cracked and thunder roared, but the midwife worked unperturbed. And as she worked, she remembered that tragic night in the same cabin thirteen years earlier, when she had witnessed the death of Cricket.

They named the child Clarence Walker (later known as "Nick"). He was the first-born son of the sixty-nine year-old Harvey Walker Nichols. Two other children, John and Pauline, were born during the next three years.

It was a new life for Harvey, a man whose thinning dark brown hair had turned silver and then white, a man who had come to be known in recent years as Old Man Harvey. Now he had a young wife and a new family. He was proud of himself.

109

Harvey Nichols with his son Clarence "Nick" in front of the Jones Mountain Cabin, July 1936. Roof of springhouse is visible at right. The garden shown here was the last one Harvey planted on Jones Mountain. Within a year, the land had become part of Shenandoah National Park. Path beyond the springhouse went into the woods, passed through another field, and led to a stream in another hollow, where Harvey often operated his still.

110

The Last Years on Jones Mountain

At age seventy, Harvey still had a reputation for bull strength and stamina. Charles Jenkins saw him pick up a 196-pound barrel of flour and walk away. Another man saw him pick up a 100-pound sack of feed without moving his feet. "Oh, Lord, that man was strong!" Homer Shifflett said.

Harvey also had a reputation as an expert weather forecaster. One day he studied the signs, then climbed down to the Staunton River to warn people of an approaching storm.

"Put up your stock. It's going to snow tonight," Harvey told them.

Will Shifflett thought Harvey had lost his mind. "It isn't going to snow tonight, Harvey. It's too cold," he said.

But Harvey knew what he knew. He scrambled back to the Jones Mountain Cabin and made ready for a storm. That night, a howling wind charged up the slopes, and snow started falling. It came down heavily for several hours, reaching a depth of sixteen inches by dawn.

In his later years, Harvey still hiked the trails, though now he frequently carried a staff. One staff in particular became a topic of conversation throughout the area. He cut it from a branch of a willow tree one spring while hiking down Big Kinsey Hollow. Later, upon reaching the old slave church near Graves Mill, he stopped at a spring, pushed the end of the stick into the ground, then knelt and drank from the pool of water. Walking on, he forgot about the staff, which remained upright in the ground. Within a few days, the fresh willow staff took root and eventually grew into a tree.

"Harvey Nichols' walking cane." The tree sprouted from a fresh willow staff that Harvey pushed into the ground when he paused to get a drink of water. The tree died in the 1970s.

Despite the good times, trouble was on its way for Harvey Nichols. Back in the 1920s he had heard the rumors about the new national park that would be taking over the Blue Ridge Mountains. Then the news came that Bear Church and Harvey's cabin would be included in the park.

When Harvey heard the news, he felt the deep gravity of depression. Harvey's life and works, his memories, his dreams and hopes were on Jones Mountain. And now the National Park Service, an organization that Harvey had never heard of, was going to take over the mountain and move him away.

Harvey walked alone on the trails, and then he told Lady that he would not leave. No one could make him leave Jones Mountain. He was going to stay.

For months, Harvey waited. Then one day, a government man came down the trail. He was tall, dressed in clean, well-pressed clothes. He told Harvey about the new Shenandoah National Park and said that the park would have to take Harvey's land. "We must buy your land, and we'll have to burn the house."

Harvey stared at the man in disbelief. "If you take this place, I won't live much longer," he said. "This is all I have ever had, and I don't have the strength to start all over."

The agent told Harvey that the decision had already been made. If necessary, the government would evict him by force. "You've got to get out of here, Mr. Nichols," he warned.

"I'm not leaving," Harvey said. "I'm not going anywhere."

But after several months, Harvey sadly accepted the reality of what was happening to his life on Jones Mountain. He was paid $8.33 an acre for the land and the buildings, and then he made ready to leave.

"After Harvey left, he never went back to the cabin," neighbor Marie Shifflett said.

The Abandoned Cabin

In the old days, when thirty-five acres of open fields surrounded Harvey Nichols' cabin, people could see the structure from the Goodall farm on the Rapidan River. So when Harvey moved from the cabin in 1937, the valley farmers often looked up at the site, expecting at any time to see the cabin and sheds go up in smoke. National park rangers were burning and destroying all the former dwellings and farm buildings in the area, and now the time had come for the burning of Harvey Nichols' cabin.

But what surprised everyone was that Harvey's cabin never burned, and strangely, the people of Graves Mill sometimes saw lights on the mountain at night. Someone eventually climbed up to investigate and found that hikers were camping there.

"Hikers from Washington went up there to Harvey's cabin after he sold," Effie McDaniel said. "It was just for a while after Harvey left. The hikers went up there, and everyone always wondered why the park didn't burn Harvey's cabin."

Pauline Nichols at fourteen; daughter of Harvey and Lady Nichols.

Harvey Nichols, three years after he moved from the Jones Mountain Cabin.

Minnie Nichols Hess, fourth daughter of Harvey and Lady Nichols, lived in the Jones Mountain Cabin for 15 years. She is pictured here during interview with author 55 years later.

113

Kentuck Mountain

Harvey and Lady lived for a few weeks in the Lillard house on the Staunton River, owned then by friend Tom Lillard, the sheriff of Madison County. Then, when that house was also closed, Harvey and Lady once more moved on. They were offered a house in a resettlement area near Wolftown but turned it down. Harvey chose instead to move to the top of Kentuck Mountain near Flattop Ridge, high above Graves Mill, where Silas Flinchem had built a log cabin.

"Old Man Harvey still wanted to live on a mountain," Charles Jenkins said.

Deputy Sheriff Hume Lillard helped Harvey move. "It took four horses to get the wagon up that steep grade to the top of Kentuck," Hume said.

It wasn't long before Harvey adjusted to his new surroundings. Within a few weeks, he was drawing whiskey from the copper still, and Harvey's Special again went on sale. "Dad kept the still chained to a walnut tree on Kentuck," son Nick said. "He kept some of the equipment hid in a wall, a secret compartment in a wall at the springhouse."

But times were changing. "When the park came, the law was too close, and almost all of the moonshining stopped," Charles Jenkins said. "Old Man Harvey kept on making it, but the rest of it stopped."

Charles Jenkins was right. The law was close. One day during the fifty-fifth year of Harvey's moonshining, government agents roared down the road from Wolftown, swept suddenly across Kentuck Mountain, located and seized the still, and placed Harvey Nichols under arrest.

But the court apparently just winked at the violation. The judge let Harvey off. He put him on probation, and Harvey returned to Kentuck Mountain. Predictably, he rebuilt the still, and for the rest of his life Harvey continued making and selling whiskey and brandy.

In 1941, Harvey and Lady moved again, this time down the mountain into a back hollow of Kentuck, where he built a small frame house. From the new location, son Nick walked to school at Graves Mill. "Harvey moved down from the mountain so his children could get an education," Dewey Shifflett said.

It was a cold, wet day, and the rain continued to fall. Mud was deep on the roads near Graves Mill. That morning, Frank Jarrell was in the store when he looked up to see Lady Nichols walk in, a look of distress across her face. "Harvey is dead!" she cried.

Harvey Walker Nichols died suddenly at nine o'clock that morning, March 28, 1944. It was his seventy-eighth birthday. Harvey had not been ill, but for several days he had complained of chest pains. He did not go to a doctor.

Claude McDaniel took in horses and a sled and brought out the body. The coffin was placed in the Graves Chapel for two days while people came to pay their last respects to the grand old man of Jones Mountain. There was no funeral service.

The rain continued for three days but let up briefly the day of the burial. While friends and the family gathered, undertaker Haywood Hood and several pallbearers buried Harvey in a small family cemetery in the south foothills of Jones Mountain. He was buried beside his mother and father and his sister Comora.

"We didn't have a minister," Charles Jenkins said. "We just brought Harvey up here and buried him."

Fieldstone marks the grave of Harvey Nichols.

Part III

The National Park

The land slept under a
Thin blanket of late January snow.
The mountains were shrouded
In a gray effervescent lowering sky.
And the silence was like
Pure music from distant stars.

"The Quiet Land"
by V.E. Townsend

In the gathering dusk of an autumn evening in 1937, five men sat on Bear Church Rock and looked out on the heights and depths of the Blue Ridge Mountains in the new Shenandoah National Park. The wild and rugged Staunton River valley stretched out below. In the distance, the bronze outlines of Doubletop and Fork Mountain loomed in a thin haze.

One man was playing a harmonica and another was smoking a pipe. "We liked to sit there on Bear Church Rock in the evenings when we were staying at the cabin," hiker Harris Shettel said. "We would walk up there and spend the evenings, and we would sit there on the rock and watch the day end and look down on the Staunton River."

Night had fallen when the five men left Bear Church Rock. They descended steeply down a dark gulf to an old wagon trail below an open field, then followed the trail along a rail fence beside a dense thicket of laurel. After passing through a drawbar gate at a trailhead, they dropped down to another open field on a promontory and circled back into a small hollow, where they came to the recently vacated cabin of mountaineer Harvey Nichols.

The men climbed a step ladder to the main floor of the cabin, where their food and gear were stored. Hot coals glowed in the large stone fireplace at one end of the room. They rekindled the fire, cooked a meal of beans and ham, and settled back to eat by the light of the fire. Then they brewed coffee and talked into the night about Jones Mountain and the old trails they had found. Later, they brought out their bedrolls and bedded down in front of the fireplace.

The Trail Blazers

The five men who slept at Harvey Nichols' cabin that night were pioneer trail builders of the Potomac Appalachian Trail Club (PATC). They had come to the back country of the new national park to clear and blaze hiking trails connecting to the Appalachian Trail, five miles away on Hazeltop Mountain.

One of the five, Dr. William A. Turner, had found the cabin a few weeks earlier while exploring the mountain range east of the Laurel Prong. Bill Turner was a loner with a yearning for wilderness. And in the course of time, he bushwhacked his way to the bluegrass field in the basin above Garth Spring, then picked up the Jones Mountain Trail and followed it across the tableland to the rock ridge and on down into the hollow, where he discovered the Jones Mountain Cabin. Harvey Nichols had been gone just a few weeks.

Bill Turner contacted Harris Shettel, a veteran outdoorsman and trail expert who worked every weekend on PATC's trails. Shortly thereafter, the two men packed their duffel and set out for Jones Mountain.

"The cabin was in very good condition, made of huge chestnut logs with siding," Harris Shettel said. "There was a spring out front. Down below the spring there was a pen, probably a hog pen, and the pen was enclosed with one-inch boards made of solid walnut. I remember thinking those boards would make a nice tabletop."

Bill Turner and Harris Shettel had started on a project just a year earlier to clear a network of hiking trails to scenic points on the high mountain land above the old Hoover camp. They recruited three friends to help break the trails.

George Betz, the pipe smoker, was a natural choice. He and Harris Shettel hobnobbed together and were co-overseers of the Appalachian Trail south of Old Forge Camp in Pennsylvania. Both men were metalworkers by trade. The harmonica player was Dr. Charles Woodward, a professor of astronomy and an avid outdoorsman. A hiker named Wiseman was the fifth member of the group.

In the previous year, the five men had worked from a base camp at the edge of the old Adam Hurt Field near the Sag. "We camped off the fire road near some trees, where there was a small clearing," Shettel said. "There was a swamp area down farther in the hemlocks near a bed of trilliums, and we got our water down there in big cans and hauled it up to where we camped."

The trail workers recleared and blazed the route from Hoover's camp up to the Sag, then cleared an obsure trail that Turner had found leading to Cat Knob and down to Laurel Gap. From the gap, they cleared the old Hoover trail to the summit of Hazeltop, where they connected with the Appalachian Trail. "We used a dark shade of blue paint to blaze the trails," Harris Shettel said. It was paint that would remain on some of the trees for forty-one years.

The new trails were formally inaugurated two weeks later, on June 28, 1936, when Clark Dean of PATC led the first organized hike in the Jones Mountain area. Five days later, on July 3, another dedication took place just three miles to the northwest. President Franklin D. Roosevelt came in a motorcade up Skyline Drive to Big Meadows, where a crowd of five thousand people gathered for the formal dedication of Shenandoah National Park.

Then came 1937, when Bill Turner discovered the recently vacated Nichols cabin. Turner and Shettel drew up plans to clear a trail to the area and open the cabin for hikers. They also decided to open hiking trails in the Staunton River Valley and on Jones Mountain connecting with the new Cat Knob network and the Appalachian Trail.

"We figured there would be a lot of people using that area and the Staunton creek," Harris said.

The National Park Service approved the plan for the trails but turned down the proposal to open the Jones Mountain Cabin.

"They wanted to burn the cabin!" Harris Shettel said indignantly. "They wanted to destroy it! They didn't want to leave anything there. And we argued and fought. We told them they ought to leave that cabin stand."

The PATC members won the fight. "We convinced the park that the cabin should stay for hikers coming down from Bear Church Rock," said Shettel.

The volunteer trail gang used the cabin as a base camp for six work trips while they cleared and blazed the Jones Mountain trails. They drove up the Fork Mountain Fire Road and parked across from Bear Church Rock, then followed the Ward-Rue trail down to the Staunton River and climbed Jones Mountain on the old wagon trail.

In the fall of 1937, the PATC crew recleared and blue-blazed what is now the McDaniel Hollow Trail, then recut and blazed the high trail to Bear Church Rock, where they went for their evening jaunts. On succeeding work trips, they made their way along the old trail on the crest of Jones Mountain, out past the bluegrass field and on toward Cat Knob. "There was a trail up there, but it was almost obscure when we got there," Shettel said.

"One time in the autumn, we were up there on the top of Jones Mountain where it was flat, and we worked till dark. The moon came up, a full moon, and we never saw such a picture in all our lives-the outline of the landscape and the trees, with the moon in the background.

"And we were having such a good time working on the trail and looking at the scenery. But then we realized it was late! By gosh, we had to get down off that mountain! But nobody wanted to leave. We enjoyed that view so much. And we worked up there on the mountain till nine o'clock. The evenings weren't too long in the fall, and so we had to find our way back to the cabin in the dark."

In the weeks that followed, the five volunteers cut and blazed the trail all the way to Cat Knob. Then they recleared the old trail up through the hemlocks to the Sag. And then the job was finished.

121

Unknown to the PATC trail workers, they had reopened and blazed most of Harvey Nichols' favorite hunting trail, the eight-mile circuit. The trails leading to the Hoover camp and Hazeltop brought the total to twelve miles of blue-blazed trails, completed by the early winter of 1937.

About the same time that the Turner party labored on Jones Mountain, another pionéer of the Potomac Appalachian Trail Club was at work nearby on the peaks and ridges north of the Rapidan. Trailblazer Charles P. Thomas, a friend of Harris Shettel, cleared and blazed a five-mile ridge-top trail on Doubletop and Chapman Mountains, beginning at the Big Bridge on the Rapidan River just east of Jones Mountain. The trail ascended to the top of Chapman Mountain on the former Criglersville Road, then passed near the former homesite of the McDaniels, where part of the family had lived for some fifty years after the Staunton River home had burned.

Charley Thomas' trail then extended northwesterly along the broken crest of Doubletop and followed a graded trail on the south slopes that the Civilian Conservation Corps (CCC) had just built near the former Knighting home. The trail ended at Broyles Gap.

Charley finished his trail in the fall of 1936. Hikers hailed the new pathway. PATC Supervisor of Trails Frank Schairer said that Charley's new trail would "provide the hiker with almost every variety of trail . . .

Volunteer trail workers of the Potomac Appalachian Trail Club (PATC) at their camp on the edge of the Adam Hurt Field near the Sag, June 1936. These men were credited with saving the Jones Mountain Cabin. Left to right, Dr. Charles Woodward, a hiker named Wiseman, Harris Shettel, and George Betz. Photo was made by Dr. William Turner, the leader.

as well as with splendid views from the three summits and other outlooks.''

Frank Schairer also commended the Turner group. The Jones Mountain trails became popular destinations for hikers during the late 1930s. Bill Turner himself led a group of sixty-nine hikers to the trails on a warm sunny, autumn day in 1939. The group split at Cat Knob, one part going directly to the Sag while the others hiked the mountaintop to Bear Church Rock, then had lunch at Harvey Nichols' cabin.

Hiker Sam Moore was with the group that day. "We stopped for a long rest at the Rock, then dropped down to the Staunton," he recalled. "Turner had the trails in pretty good condition, but the hemlock area was rough." Hiker Madeline Haenny recorded in her journal that the Nichols cabin was "a deluxe edition of an abandoned mountaineer's cabin."

In 1938, the National Park Service constructed a new trail through rock outcrops along the side of Hazeltop Ridge connecting Laurel Gap with the Appalachian Trail near Bootens Gap. The Park Service then closed Turner's blue-blazed route (formerly Hoover's horse trail) to the summit of Hazeltop. In 1939, Park Service crews cut a new trail from Milam Gap down the Mill Prong to Big Rock Falls and the Hoover camp. The new footpath would become known as the Mill Prong Trail. The upper half mile of the footpath followed the old pioneer road that Harvey Nichols had walked during his courting days.

The World War II Years

After 1939, interest in the Jones Mountain trails began to decline. In 1940, few hikers explored the remote reaches of Jones Mountain, and by 1941 most of the trails were faint or nonexistent.

For a few years, PATC trail workers continued to maintain the short McDaniel Hollow Trail and the Cat Knob link, repainting the dark blue blazes with a lighter shade. But eventually, all of the trails east of the Laurel Prong were abandoned. The same fate came to Charley Thomas' blue-blazed trail on Doubletop and Chapman Mountain.

During the Second World War, gasoline rationing and wartime jobs put the mountains out of reach for most people. The old pathways grew up in weeds. Fallen trees and branches blocked the way. And in time, the trails were gone and forgotten.

Harris Shettel mourned: "We thought people would want to hike Jones Mountain and go down to the cabin. But to my knowledge, not one soul ever hiked down those trails to stay overnight at the cabin."

During the war years, Jones Mountain was not without activity. U.S. Army troops bivouacked in the Staunton River valley for several months in 1943, when the army set up an alpine training camp in preparation for the invasion of Italy. Military police closed off the mountains to civilians as large troop convoys passed back and forth through Graves Mill. During the summer and fall, the troops regularly stormed Jones Mountain as part of their alpine war exercises.

Army engineers rebuilt and partly relocated the old wagon road along the Staunton River. To stabilize the road surface, they pushed over most of the old rock retaining walls that had lined the road for a century, then embedded the stone using rock crushers mounted on the front of jeeps. Only two short sections of the wall remained intact, one in the lower valley and the other nearly two miles up the river. The engineers also constructed drainage ditches, wood culverts, and small bridges. Machine gun nests were constructed along the mountainside. No buildings were constructed, since the training camp was a bivouac in which only military tents and mobile vans were used.

The last of the troops pulled out in the fall of 1943, leaving Jones Mountain to the Graves Mill farmers, who poked through the abandoned camp. The newspapers carried the stories of the invasion, as the mountain-trained U.S. troops landed at Oran, Italy, on the Gulf of Salerno in September 1943 and at Anzio beach in January 1944. Later, they swept north through the rugged foothills of the Italian Alps.

The ending of World War II in 1945 did not bring a revival of interest in the Jones Mountain area. The old blue-blazed trails were dropped from the map in 1946, when the Potomac Appalachian Trail Club published an updated map of the central section of the Shenandoah National Park. The trails were shown as unmarked bushwhack routes. Later editions of PATC's maps dropped the trails entirely.

The years passed, and the Jones Mountain trails were buried in time and grown over by new forests.

"Our work was all for naught," lamented Harris Shettel.

The Bushwhackers

In the 1960s, it was said that there used to be trails on Jones Mountain. But stories were told of people getting lost, and few people ventured beyond the Laurel Prong. On rare occasions bushwhackers found their way into the rugged back country to explore animal trails and logging routes obscured by brush and fallen trees.

James W. Denton of Front Royal, Virginia, was one of the explorers. On a clear, cold day in the twenty-fourth winter after the Jones Mountain trails were abandoned, Denton drove along Skyline Drive. He looked off toward the distant mountain range above the Conway River, when he caught a glimpse of what seemed to be an old trail or road up the side of a mountain.

"There was snow on the ground, and just for an instant I saw a clear line of snow that seemed to mark a trail," he said.

Denton parked his car at Bootens Gap and walked down the Conway Fire Road to a point beside Bootens Run. Then he climbed the south side of Jones Mountain, where eventually he found a trail. "It looked like a logging road," he remembered. I followed it to near the top of the mountain, where two old roads branched off." Denton had been following a logging trail that coincided in places with the old Bootens Run (sometimes called Middle River) Trail of the early 1800s, the same trail Harvey Nichols had walked en route to the Devils Ditch and the trail Rosa Taylor had climbed when she assisted Cricket and Lady in childbirth.

Jim Denton bushwhacked through scrubwood, then climbed a steep pitch to the crest of the mountain, where he came to another obscure trail. He had found the old Jones Mountain Trail. Jim followed the dim path across the tableland and made his way through a thicket of brush and small trees, once the Garth Spring Field. He followed the ridge on out to Bear Church Rock, where he found an aging weathered sign marked PATC, indicating the direction to the Staunton River. He headed down this route, eventually coming to McDaniel Hollow, then climbed up through the Wilderness to the Sag and Cat Knob and headed back to his car. "There were some remains of old blazes on trees up there near Cat Knob and along the top of Jones Mountain," he said.

On October 20, 1963, Jim Denton returned to Jones Mountain with a large group of hikers. They followed his earlier route from the Conway River up through scrubwood to the dim trail that led to Bear Church Rock. "It was rough," said veteran hiker Frank Shelburne.

Rediscovery

Old-timers said there was a cabin somewhere up on Jones Mountain, where an early pioneer had lived. Some said he was a moonshiner, but all spoke of him with reverence, and the stories captured the imagination of hikers.

A few hikers searched for the cabin. Jim Denton and Frank Shelburne tried in early 1968. "We came up the Staunton River and climbed through snow to Bear Church Rock," Shelburne said.

Jim Denton dropped down into the hollow below the Rock, where he broke through laurel and came eventually to a sunlit area of heavy undergrowth. "I thought the cabin might be in there somewhere, but I couldn't see it," he said. In fact, he was standing near the cabin in one of the grown-over fields.

About the same time, bushwhacker Woody Kennedy led hiker Howard Brackney on a winter excursion to the Staunton River area. They headed for the wilds of Bear Church Rock but encountered ice on the low road. Woody pressed on, carrying seventy pounds of gear. But near the Rapidan he slipped on a sheet of ice and fell hard, breaking two ribs. "Woody was flattened out, face down, on the hard ice," Howard Brackney said.

Woody and Howard backtracked, then made camp about thirty feet from the raging Rapidan River. The temperature was nineteen degrees. Snow began falling, and the two men huddled over a campfire. A stray dog came by and stayed with them for the rest of the night.

The next morning, Howard carried Woody's gear out across Chapman Mountain. "That was not one of my great hikes," the usually robust Woody Kennedy said.

The two hikers never made it to Bear Church Rock, but the call of Jones Mountain was irresistible to Howard Brackney, and he returned just two weeks later. "I was inspired by Woody's description of the view from Bear Church Rock," he said.

It was another cold day. Brackney was accompanied this time by backpackers Art Douglas and Larry Smith. They climbed above the river, then separated. Douglas scrambled up to Bear Church Rock while Smith and Brackney searched for a spring and a suitable place to camp.

"I had planned a camp-out knowing nothing about the area except what Woody Kennedy had told me and what I could learn from one of Egbert Walker's old [PATC] maps. It was on an old, out-of-date issue of this map that I recalled having seen a spring indicated in the ravine below and east of the Rock," Howard Brackney said. "Larry Smith went up the hollow in the direction of the Rock. I went straight down into the hollow following an old path, and to my amazement I came upon what looked like a mountaineer's cabin of unusual quality. Nearby, I found a spring."

Howard Brackney had discovered Harvey Nichols' cabin. The date was Saturday, February 24, 1968.

Meanwhile, Larry Smith had glimpsed the structure from afar. "It was like an apparition, like a camera coming into focus," he recalled.

"We slept in the cabin and even had a fire in the fireplace," Larry Smith said. That night, the temperature dropped to thirteen degrees.

The next morning, the hikers examined the old structure. Unoccupied for thirty-one years, the cabin was still in fair condition. Part of the roof had caved in, but the massive chimney and the logs were well preserved. The workmanship was exceptional. The upper floor and rafters were weathered, but the beams and lower floor were solid.

Harvey's old springhouse was standing. The sheds above the cabin were in good condition. The rail gateway at the old trailhead was in place. The entire area was overgrown with saplings, vines, and persimmon trees.

"We were struck by the possibilities of restoring the cabin and thought it would be a good project for PATC," Howard Brackney said.

Photo by Fred Blackburn.

Jones Mountain Cabin, March 10, 1968. John Oliphant (left) and Howard Brackney in doorway.

On March 10, Brackney again climbed to the Jones Mountain cabin. This time, he brought John L. Oliphant, the president of the Potomac Appalachian Trail Club, and Fred Blackburn, a key member. Howard Brackney's enthusiasm carried the day. That evening, John Oliphant headed home to Washington, where he formulated plans to reopen the cabin.

John Oliphant told Taylor Hoskins, superintendent of Shenandoah National Park, about the discovery. Then on May 6, Oliphant tracked up the mountain with Hoskins to inspect the cabin. Accompanying them were PATC Supervisor of Trails Ray Fadner and Bob Humphrey, a specialist in cabin restoration. Taylor Hoskins was impressed, and in early July he approved the proposal to restore and preserve the pioneer cabin.

But that year, because the club's cabin builders were busy near Ramsey Draft constructing another cabin, the project on Jones Mountain was delayed. As the time drew on, Howard Brackney became impatient. "I prodded them unmercifully to get going," he said.

Restoration of the Jones Mountain Cabin

Work on the Jones Mountain Cabin restoration started on July 19, 1969. Expert builder Bob Humphrey was in charge.

The first problem was figuring out how to get the materials to the remote mountain site. "The old trails were practically nonexistent," Humphrey said. "The old road along the Staunton River was blocked by deadfalls and washouts. Trees had fallen everywhere." There was not a trace of Bush Field or the old meadows of the lower valley. The entire area had long ago returned to forest.

Bob Humphrey eventually found Harvey Nichols' old wagon trail. "The area was heavily overgrown. We could barely see the embankment at the bottom where the trail started and the cut at the top where it ended, but in between it was hard to follow. On top, mountain laurel had grown over the trail. It was surely a lost trail."

Rain, heat, and humidity limited the work that first day, but seventeen workers cleared a mile of the Staunton River road. Late that day, they made camp on a level stretch of the road. "We camped right where we dropped," Bob Humphrey said. A plastic sheet as large as a circus tent was hoisted for shelter.

"That night, the mosquitoes ate us up," Bill Amtmann said.

Sunday broke clear and sunny, and the volunteers forged on, cutting through dense growth and fallen trees. Several workers wielded picks and shovels, repairing washouts.

Fred Blackburn starting work on the porch during the restoration of the Jones Mountain Cabin, about 1970.

Volunteer workers during the restoration of the cabin, 1971.

One man in the group was puzzled by the wood culverts and bridges left there by the army in 1943. "Somebody years ago had built some wooden culverts, and they were all caved in," Bill Amtmann said. The work gang excavated the culverts and installed fifteen-foot-long sewer pipes made of asbestos cement.

While digging in the backfill of one old culvert, Bill Amtmann found a 1930 automobile license tag with one number rusted out. It was a Virginia tag, number 26(?)-194. "That tag had lasted thirty-nine years in a damp environment. It was obviously not a low-carbon steel. They don't make steel like that anymore," he said.

The work crew came at length to the old chestnut tree, seven feet across, that had been a landmark in the valley during the early twentieth century. Killed by the blight, it had fallen across the road and now blocked the passage of Amtmann's four-wheel-drive vehicle. A chain saw was brought in later to cut through the giant tree.

Several members of the crew stayed on to clear more of the road, but most of the workers returned home early the second day to watch television, which featured the first landing of a man on the moon.

In the weeks that followed, the workers opened the Staunton River road two miles, then cleared the Nichols' wagon road to a turnaround below Bear Church Rock. The remaining half mile was cleared for foot travel only.

Bill Amtmann and Bill Oscanyon used jeeps to haul in 1,800 pounds of roofing shingles, 960 pounds of cement, and several loads of lumber and other supplies. Work crews carried the materials by hand the last half mile.

In the fall of 1969, Bob Humphrey's crew ripped out the old rafters and the roof, and by December they had installed a new roof with a skylight opening.

For the next four years, work progressed slowly as Bob Humphrey engineered the restoration with meticulous care. About six work trips were scheduled each year. Regular participants included Bob Phillips and Bill Opdyke, who were named as overseers of the cabin. Others were Fred and Ruth Blackburn, Paula Strain, Diana Niskern, Bob Wolf, Dick Jachowski, Evan Gull, and Lowell Goodson. Howard Brackney helped transport the materials and occasionally accompanied the cabin crew.

The workers removed Harvey's old springhouse and the two sheds. The old barn had burned down years earlier. Logs from the cow shed were used in the construction of a new porch on the cabin. The chimney and foundation were stabilized and repointed. Bob Humphrey cut out part of the attic floor to create a loft opening above the fireplace. He also

The restored Jones Mountain Cabin.

Harvey's son Nick Nichols sitting in the cabin in which he was born. Nick's grandfather Albert built the fireplace about 1855. Photo by the author was made in 1979 during Nick's first visit to the cabin since his parents left, when he was two years old.

added a double window to the second floor. Final work included install-ing cabinets, two bunks, and a potbellied stove. Bob also blazed the three-mile access trail from the Rapidan River near the edge of the na-tional park.

Not all of the crew's time was spent working. They explored the old Staunton River Road past North New Ground to Hundleys Ford, an area that had become heavily forested. The crew usually had a campfire in the evenings. Sometimes the workers hiked late in the day to Wild Hog Rock, which they called Humphrey Rock, where they viewed the Staunton River Valley and the low knobs of Fork Mountain. Howard Brackney climbed past the overlook to Bear Church Rock, then headed along an old trail to the ragged, picturesque summit of Bluff Mountain, part of the Rapidan Wildlife Management Area.

"Our people liked to hike and camp, but we didn't have too much time for that sort of thing," Bob Humphrey said. "Most of our people were sacked out by eight-thirty."

The cabin workers completed the restoration on June 2, 1974, when the structure was dedicated as Jones Mountain Cabin. Despite heavy fog and drizzle, forty-nine people attended the ceremony, which was held in-doors around the fireplace. Some people watched from the loft balcony. Among those present were Humphrey, who described the project, and PATC President Bob Wolf, who praised the work crew. Darwin Lambert, nationally known writer who in 1936 had been the first Park Service employee in the new Shenandoah National Park, spoke about the early history and folklore of the mountains.

Later, the cabin was opened as a rental unit available to backpackers by reservation. A parking area was cleared three miles away near the old Brown Camp at the confluence of the Rapidan and the Staunton.

Wildlife Returns to the Mountain

During the year in which the cabin restoration was completed, mountain lions were sighted on Jones Mountain, the first observations in more than a century. Charles Jenkins encountered a cougar about two miles from the Jones Mountain Cabin. The big cat came down the moun-tain to Jenkins' farm twice, flustering livestock. Six months later, James McDaniel saw a cougar above Big Kinsey Hollow. About the same time, hiker Jim Denton encountered a mountain lion below Jones Mountain near the Laurel Prong.

Other wildlife was making a comeback in the woodland frontier around Jones Mountain. Deer, wild turkeys, and bears had returned to the area in recent years. Bears were seen near Bear Church Rock and Bear Hunting Ridge after an absence of some one hundred years.

In the adjoining seven-thousand acre Rapidan Wildlife Management Area, sports hunting increased dramatically. In the fall of the year, jeeps and big trucks rumbled up the fire roads carrying hunters with sleek, high-powered rifles. One year, twenty-eight bears were killed in Madison County, almost all of them in the Rapidan Wildlife Management Area. The county led the state in bear kills for two consecutive years.

Fishing increased on the Rapidan and Staunton Rivers. Gone were the days of Harvey Nichols and Will Shifflett, when only five or six men fished the old Wilson Run. Now located entirely within the national park, the Staunton River became famous as a classic eastern trout stream with its rock crevices and shallow riffles. It was one of the few remaining habitats in the area for native brook trout. Fishing pressure on the stream eventually resulted in fish-for-fun rules, which required anglers to release their catches.

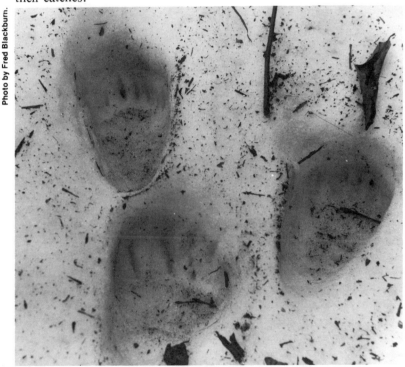

Bear tracks in snow near Jones Mountain Cabin, 1968.

Hikers and Trail Builders

In the early 1970s, hikers along the Appalachian Trail began talking about the pioneer cabin on Jones Mountain. They often came down the Mill Prong and Laurel Prong Trails to the deep rhododendron valley below the Sag, but few of the hikers attempted to cross Jones Mountain.

In the spring of 1972, the Wanderbirds Hiking Club sent scouts into the mountains to find a trail for a group excursion that the club wanted to to sponsor. The leader was Frank Shelburne, the veteran of the Denton hikes in 1963 and 1968. "Cat Knob was very hard to find," Shelburne recalled. "I got Oliver and Carol Flint, Dave Brownlie, Dave Schlain, and Jim Denton, and we cleared out a trail along the top of Jones Mountain."

They followed the old Jones Mountain Trail, most of which had nearly vanished. "We climbed up there five of six times for work trips," Shelburne said. "It was tricky country. If you went off the trail far, the only way you could find your way back was by shouting to your friends on the trail."

They finished the job, and on November 5, 1972, Shelburne and Wendy Lobdell led the excursion across Jones Mountain for the Wanderbirds Club. In 1973, they led another group through the same area for the Potomac Appalchian Trail Club. Later that year, Wendy Lobdell guided the Capital Hiking Club along the ridge-top route. On all three occasions, PATC member Connie Carter escorted the hikers to the Nichols cabin, where the restoration project was in progress.

Eventually, PATC Supervisor of Trails Ray Fadner decided to blaze a footpath through the area, connecting the restored cabin to the Appalachian Trail. Park Superintendent Robert Jacobsen approved the project. In 1975, Frank Shelburne and Jed Tucker flagged a route following the Wanderbirds trail from the cabin across Bear Church Rock to Laurel Gap.

Trail construction began on November 20, 1976. The cabin was used as a base camp. The trail gang included Jack Kiernan, Barbara Hoffman, Kathy Johnston, Becky Field, Randy Saliga, Warren Sharp, Bob Davis, and Clifford Firestone, all regular members of the PATC trail crews. Starting at a new trailhead above the cabin, the workers constructed a switchback trail through thick laurel and large stone outcrops. Bypassing the original steep ascent, they slabbed up the south side of the mountain to Bear Church Rock.

They worked ten days during a twenty-one-day period, including the long Thanksgiving weekend, when fourteen trail workers wielded pick mattocks for the final ascent to the mountaintop. They also excavated a new footway through Walnut Hollow connecting to the old McDaniel road. The path became known as the McDaniel Hollow Trail.

Occasionally in the evening, they climbed to Bear Church Rock to witness the last light of the day, just as Bill Turner's group had done nearly forty years earlier. On a typical evening at the cabin, the workers ate an ample supper served with burgundy, then sang folk ballads accompanied with guitars and harmonicas. One evening at the fireside, they listened to a memorable encore as the musicians played a soft and moving rendition of "Shenandoah." On another evening, they heard Dr. Clifford Firestone recite "Jabberwock" in German and English.

The job of completing the trails went to the new overseers Bob Davis, Richard Crisci, and Nancy Butters. In early 1977, Richard Crisci and Nancy Butters flagged and then cleared a pathway up the Staunton River Valley to the Sag and down the old Hoover riding trail to the Laurel Prong. Through the giant hemlocks of the Wilderness, there was not a trace of the old trail that went back in time to the early 1800s.

Bob Davis worked several weekends in the cold winter of 1976 and 1977 reclearing the old Jones Mountain Trail. Helping were several other workers, including his daughters Leslie and Robin and PATC trail builder Warren Sharp. By nature, Bob Davis belonged to the mountains. He had Harvey Nichols' ability as a woodsman and animal tracker and a knack for mountain cookery. On one work trip, Davis spotted an owl and two foxes. Later, he tracked a bobcat.

A fox was one of the first animals to use the new trail to Bear Church Rock, as Bob Davis recorded in his journal for January 1977: "Temperatures were in the 30s both days with clear sky. There were high winds on the 20th. That morning, we followed the tracks of a fox up the new trail and into rocks along the crest of the mountain. Coming back that evening, we found that the fox had preceded us back down the trail."

Bob Davis made his biggest hit among the trail workers with his culinary skills. He was assigned as cook on one trip, when the volunteers were building the Bear Church Rock trail. For supper on Saturday night, he put together a meal of beans and ham hock, turnip greens, and mustard greens with currants and nuts. For breakfast, he cooked sourdough flapjacks and sausage.

To complete the trail project, the workers established a base camp near the Sag. While camping there on June 26 and 27, 1977, they reopened and blazed the old route to Cat Knob. One member of the crew discovered the faint blue blazes of an earlier era. And beneath the cracked paint, he saw a darker shade of blue, put there by the Turner party in 1936.

The workers pitched camp close to where the Turner group had camped forty-one years earlier. The coincidence went further. The new trails of the 1970s followed the approximate routes that Turner's group had blazed in the 1930s. Both groups blazed about twelve miles of trails, ten of which coincided. The trail workers of the 1970s had no knowledge that they were following the route of an earlier crew, just as Bill Turner's crew had no knowlege that they were following Harvey Nichols' hunting trails.

Bob Davis and daughter Robin work on the trail to Cat Knob.

136

The Shadow of History

Hikers began exploring the new trails shortly after the footpaths were marked. A few excursion leaders brought groups to the area, but most hikers came in small groups or alone, usually while staying at the cabin. In 1978, the National Park Service installed concrete directional posts at trailheads and intersections. A new guidebook to back-country hiking, written by Molly Denton, gave information about the new trails.

Most of the new footpaths were in Shenandoah National Park, but major segments of the Jones Mountain Trail were owned by the Virginia Game and Fish Commission and local resident Jeannie Light, who granted permission. Jeannie Light owned the seven-hundred-acre Big Kinsey Hollow tract, including the slave cemetery, the old Kinsey Distillery works, and the home site of Buck Hawkins. The tract extended across the top of Jones Mountain, close to Bear Church Rock. (In 1981, Bob Davis began the work of reopening the old trail beyond the spring at the Jones Mountain Cabin, the same trail that Harvey Nichols had sometimes used for his still operations while his daughter Maude stood watch at the cabin. The trail, most of which had disappeared, extended to Jeannie Light's land on what is today called Bear Hunting Ridge.)

In 1977, Bob Davis' assignment as overseer of the Jones Mountain Trail was expanded to include the Staunton River and Fork Mountain sections, when overseers Richard Crisci and Nancy Butters moved to Alaska. A key objective of the Potomac Appalachian Trail Club and the National Park Service was to retain the backwoods character of the trailways. The Club and the Park Service also stressed historic preservation. To these ends, Bob Davis' trail standards were made to order.

"When I think of the Jones Mountain Trail, I think of a footpath winding across the top of a wild mountain on its way back into eternity," Bob Davis said. "The trail winds back and forth between present and historical uses.

"The trails give the hiker a complete menu of ways to explore the wildness of Jones Mountain. In maintaining the trails, I try to use a light touch that is in keeping with the character of the mountain. The blazing is adequate for those who can use their woodcraft to recognize the trail and need an occasional reminder that they are still on the trail."

One day in 1979, while working on the tableland, Bob Davis left the trail and pushed through a tangle of underbrush and new forest and made his way into a broad basin, where he came at length to a high mountain spring. He had crossed into the old Garth Spring Field, now grown over, once the grazing land of John Fray's cattle.

Davis stood at Garth Spring for a while and studied the area, the same place where George Hume had stood 231 years earlier. Faint traces

Drawbar post which Harvey Nichols carved from a chestnut tree, still standing in 1981. Small peg at bottom prevented hogs and other livestock from raising the fence rail and crawling under.

of an old stock trail went down the mountain and another across the basin to the top. In the adjacent hollow, several hundred feet away, was the site of the old cabin, gone now for nearly ninety years, where young Elic McDaniel and his bride Lydia had lived. Beyond were two more tracks, one going down and the other up and across the mountain.

"The mountain has many trails like this that go off to the sides in history, but I have not tried to open them," Davis said. "I leave that for the adventurous."

Bob Davis returned to the tableland, picked up his tools, and headed off down the Jones Mountain Trail. He knew that he was walking in the shadow of history.

James "Bulga" Estes about 1855. He owned orchards on the Staunton River and forest lands extending to the top of Jones Mountain in what is today Shenandoah National Park. Estes lived near Kinsey Run. He was a judge at the Graves Mill tournament in 1876, one of the last events of its kind in the history of Virginia. Competitors in foot races ran a course north from Graves Mill following about the same route as the present-day road leading into Shenandoah Park.

The Estes farm in the Graves Mill Valley with Jones Mountain in the background. This was the home place of Ellis P. Estes in the early 1900s. His father James owned land on Jones Mountain. Original building was constructed in 1857; rebuilt in plantation style in later years. Photo by Lance O'Ferrell Estes was made in 1978.

Pewter plate from the manor house of Tom and Sarah Graves, who lived near Jones Mountain beginning in 1760.

Betty (Kite) Lillard in 1914, wife of Howard Lillard. Her son Tom Lillard served as county sheriff for 22 years.

Christine Shifflett (left) and Silva Bell Knighting at the Shifflett home on the Staunton River in 1935. Estelle Allen is standing on the porch.

Matthew "Mat" Taylor, father of Cricket and Lady
Taylor. The Taylor family lived in the remote Devils
Ditch area near what is today the Slaughter Fire
Road.

Fly rod and reel used in Jones Mountain streams for forty years.

Overgrown area in Shenandoah National Park was once a mountaintop grassland known as Garth Spring Field. Photo by author was made in 1981.

1981 photo by author shows old split-rail fence below Garth Spring in Shenandoah Park on approximate line surveyed by George Hume in 1749. Fence was built about 1920 by Will Shifflett and sons Melvin and Dewey for landowner John D. Fray.

1958 photo of Charles and Vandora (Kelly) Knighting, who met at a logging camp on Jones Mountain in the early 1920s. They settled in Ohio.

Pat Townsend in 1979 standing beside fallen remains of giant chestnut tree along the Staunton River Trail. Killed by the blight in the 1920s, the tree was the largest in the Jones Mountain Forest.

Homer and Ruby (Breeden) Shifflett in 1929. They lived in the old Lillard place on the Staunton River from 1929 to 1936. (See photo of home site on page 40.)

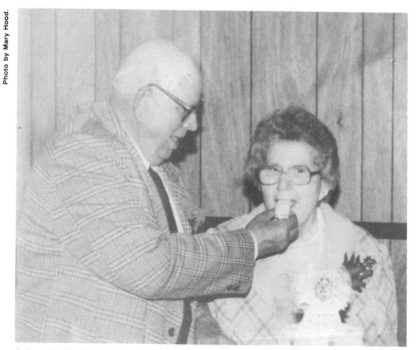

Johnnie Shifflett offers first bite of cake to wife Marie at their fiftieth wedding anniversary in 1983. They once lived in what is now Shenandoah National Park on land adjacent to mountaineer Harvey Nichols.

Chimney near the foothills of Jones Mountain marks the site of log house built in the 1890s by Albert Nichols, who earlier had built the original Jones Mountain Cabin. The Nichols family lived here at the turn of the century. Photo by author was made in 1980 shortly before the chimney was demolished.

Sources

Most of the material for this book was based on original research of land records, wills, accounts, marriage registers, court records, U.S. Census files, old plats and maps, and other archives. The genealogy of the Graves family was provided by Lois Anne Reedy. Part of the information about Graves Chapel was furnished by Fred A. Anderson, executive director of the Virginia Baptist Historical Society. Part of the information about the pre-historic Indian era was provided by Robert Evans, director of the Thunderbird Museum and Archaeological Park. Carolyn and Jack Reeder provided pertinent historical information which they researched from the records of Shenandoah National Park during the preparation of their books *Shenandoah Heritage* and *Shenandoah Vestiges.*

Credits for the oral history are, for the most part, included in the text. Quotations and most of the information relating to Buck Hawkins were taken from interviews recorded by Edward A. Bacon. Quotations by Harvey Nichols and persons with whom he conversed were provided by Minnie and Nick Nichols, Charles Jenkins, and Joe Fray. The quotation by Larry Smith was taken from the log at the Jones Mountain Cabin. Quotations by Frank Schairer and Madeline Haenny were taken from the PATC *Bulletin.* The author gratefully acknowledges contributions by the following persons, whom the author interviewed: Bill Amtmann, Melvin Aylor, Elton Berry, Fred Blackburn, Howard Brackney, Dave Brownlie, Bob Davis, Jim Denton, Lillian Allen Dickerson, Joe Fray, Minnie Nichols Hess, Mildred Hoffman, Pauline Nichols Taylor, Bob Humphrey, Frank Jarrell, Charles Jenkins, Woody Kennedy, Rosetta Taylor Lamb, Eleanor Lillard, Hume Lillard, Effie Breeden McDaniel, James E. McDaniel, Ruth McDaniel, Sam Moore, Clarence "Nick" Nichols, Sevilla Powell, Dolly Hawkins Seekford, Frank Shelburne, Harris Shettel, Clyde Shifflett, Dewey and Suzie Shifflett, Johnnie and Marie Shifflett, Homer and Ruby Shifflett, Bob Smith, and E.L. and Mildred Whitlock.

Additional information was provided by Eugene M. Scheel, Rosalie E. Davis, Haywood Hood, Jimmy and Rachel Graves, Allie Graves Wyatt, Theodore Clyde Knighting, Larry Smith, Art Douglas, Estelle Allen, and Norman Estes.

Bibliography

The following source materials provide general information about the geology of the Blue Ridge Mountains, the pre-historic period, the early settlement and folklore, the early history of Virginia and Madison County and counties in which Madison was a part during the eighteenth century, and the history of Shenandoah National Park. Davis, Dove, and Tanner include some information about the Graves Mill area.

Bean, R. Bennett. *The Peopling of Virginia,* Chapman Co., Boston, 1938.

Bradley, A.G. *Sketches from Old Virginia,* The Macmillan Co., New York, 1897.

Daniel, J.R.V. *A Hornbook of Virginia History,* The Virginia State Library, Richmond, 1965.

Davis, Margaret G. *Madison County, Virginia: A Revised History,* The Science Press, Ephrata, Pa., 1977. (First edition, Claude Yowell, Madison County Board of Supervisors, 1926.)

Dove, Vee. *Madison County Homes: A Collection of Pre-Civil War Homes and Family Heritages,* Kingsport Press, Kingsport, Tenn.

Fishback, Marshall William. *The Virginia Tradition,* Public Affairs Press, Washington, D.C., 1956.

Gathright, Thomas M. II. *Geology of the Shenandoah National Park, Virginia* Bulletin 86, Virginia Division of Mineral Resources, Charlottesville, 1976.

Huddle, Rev. W.P. *History of the Hebron Lutheran Church, from 1717 to 1907,* Henkel and Company, New Market, Va., 1908.

Lambert, Darwin. *Herbert Hoover's Hideaway: The Story of Camp Hoover on the Rapidan River in Shenandoah National Park,* Shenandoah Natural History Association, Luray, Va., 1971.

Jones, Mary Stevens. Editor. *An 18th Century Perspective: Culpeper County,* The Culpeper Historical Society, Culpeper, Va., 1976. Chapter V, contributed, "A Few of Culpeper's Outstanding 18th Century Citizens," Chapter VI, D. French Slaughter, Jr., "Thomas, Second Lord Culpeper, Baron Thorsing," Chapter VII, D. French Slaughter, Jr., "Thomas, Sixth Baron Fairfax, Baron of Cameron," Chapter VIII, Eugene M. Scheel, "Culpeper's Colonial Roads," Chapter IX, Eugene M. Scheel, "The Last Indians to Live in Culpeper," Chapter XIV, Leo S. Mason, "To Have Lived Then—the 1700's."

Lederer, John. *The Discoveries of John Lederer,* translated by Sir William Tabot, London, 1672. (University Microfilms, 1966.)

Mansfield, James Roger. *A History of Early Spotsylvania,* Orange, Va., 1977.

McCary, Ben C. *Indians in Seventeenth Century Virginia,* The Virginia 350th Anniversary Celebration Corporation, Williamsburg, 1957.

Reeder, Carolyn and Jack. *Shenandoah Heritage, The Story of the People Before the Park,* Potomac Appalachian Trail Club, Washington, D.C., 1978.
_____. *Shenandoah Vestiges, What the Mountain People Left Behind,* Potomac Appalachian Trail Club, Washington, D.C., 1980.

Rouse, Park. *Planters and Pioneers,* Hastings House, New York, 1968.

Tanner, Douglas W. *Madison County Place Names,* Virginia Place Name Society, Charlottesville, 1978.

Turner, Mary Eloise. *Way Back: Some Pioneer Ways of Olden Days,* Shenandoah Natural History Association, Luray, Va. 1973.

Sanchez-Saavedra, E.M. *A Description of the Country: Virginia's Cartographers and Their Maps, 1607-1881,* Virginia State Library, Richmond, 1975.

Wayland, John W., Editor. *The Fairfax Line: Thomas Lewis's Journal of 1746,* The Hinkel Press, New Market, Va., 1925.

Wilhelm, E.J., Jr. *The Blue Ridge: Man and Nature in Shenandoah National Park and Blue Ridge Parkway,* University of Virginia, Charlottesville, 1968.

Yowell, Claude. (See Davis, Margaret L.)

Periodicals

The various Virginia historical quarterlies contain little information directly relating to the Jones Mountain area. The most useful periodical for the area is the *Bulletin,* Potomac Appalachian Trail Club, Washington, D.C. Various issues from the 1930s to the 1970s contain information about roads, trails, and hiking in the Jones Mountain area after the establishment of Shenandoah National Park.

Maps

Culpeper County. *A Map of Culpeper County,* 1791. Prepared to accompany a proposal to form Madison County, then part of Culpeper. (Jones, Mary Stevens, *An 18th Century Perspective: Culpeper County,* p. 14. From the University of Virginia Library.)

Fry, Joshua and Peter Jefferson. *A Map of the most Inhabited part of Virginia. . .,* Commissioners of Trade and Plantations, London, 1775 (originally published in   1751).

Jefferson, Thomas. *A Map of the Country between Albemarle Sound and Lake Erie,* supplement to *Notes on the State of Virginia,* 1784.

Potomac Appalachian Trail Club. *Shenandoah National Park, Central Section,* Washington, D.C., 1931, 1938, 1941, 1944, 1946, 1950, 1955, 1962, 1965, 1969, 1975, 1980. Most of the maps were prepared by Dr. Egbert H. Walker.

Scheel, Eugene M. *A New and Accurate Map of the County of Culpeper and Regions of Madison and Rappahannock Virginia, 1776,* Warrenton, Va., 1976.

U.S. Geological Survey. *Fletcher, Virginia,* 7' quadrangle, 1965.

_____. *Madison, Virginia,* 15' quadrangle, two maps—one in color showing boundaries of proposed national park, 1933 (from surveys in 1927 and 1929-1930).

_____. *Madison, Virginia,* 7' quadrangle, 1964 (photorevised 1972).

_____. *Proposed Shenandoah National Park,* 15', 1934 (from surveys in 1927-1930).

Virginia. *A Map of the State of Virginia,* Herman Boye, 1825 (corrected 1859).

Virginia. *Index Map of Madison County,* Department of Highways, prepared to accompany *Madison County Place Names,* by Douglas W. Tanner, 1978.

Virginia. *Geologic map of the Shenandoah National Park, Central Section,* Division of Mineral Resources, geology by Thomas M. Gathright, prepared to accompany Gathright's book *Geology of the Shenandoah National Park* (1976), 1972.

Facsimiles of the maps by Fry and Boye accompany the book, *A Description of the Country,* by E.M. Sanchez-Saavedra.

INDEX

157